The Light From Above

TRUEST STORY EVER LIVED

SHARON TERBROCK

Scripture taken from The Life Application Study Bible, New International
Version, published by Tyndale House Publishers, Inc., and Zondervan
Publishing House. Copyright © 1995 by Tyndale House

Scripture taken from the King James Version of the Bible.

Inspiring Voices books may be ordered through booksellers or by contacting:

Inspiring Voices
1663 Liberty Drive
Bloomington, IN 47403
www.inspiringvoices.com
1 (866) 697-5313

ISBN: 978-1-4624-1081-1 (sc)
ISBN: 978-1-4624-1082-8 (e)

Library of Congress Control Number: 2014921692

Print information available on the last page.

Inspiring Voices rev. date: 04/27/2015

Contents

Introduction

The Truest Story Ever Lived is my poetic version of a sermon I heard one Sunday morning. The preacher covered the message of the Bible from Genesis through Revelation in less than an hour, using certain Bible passages that he had chosen. So, I went home thinking that I would try to write my own version of his sermon with the Bible verses that were used.

My version of the Bible ended up being some thirteen pages long. And while I was not able to use most of the verses he had used, I was able to use others that I hope still convey the message of God's own Word.

I pray that this story reveals our sinfulness, our wandering from God and His love. He loves us so much and wants us to turn back to Him so badly that He sent us a Savior—a Savior to live and die for us. This Savior not only taught us how to live while on this earth but also promises us a new eternal life in Him and with Him. While we will all live an eternal life, we will not all live it in the presence of God, in the presence of love. What is life without God, without love?

While I thought *The Truest Story Ever Lived* had enough content to be a small book on its own, as the book progressed I decided to add a few more of my poems. One thing led to another, and I ended up adding many of my poems to the book.

I decided to keep the title of the book as *The Truest Story Ever Lived* because, had it not been for the life of Jesus here on Earth, we would not have faith or hope in salvation or any promise of a life lived in and filled with love when we leave this world. We certainly would have no hope that would help us get through the struggles and hardships we sometimes have to endure here on this earth.

In the last few years, I wrote poems for others who were searching for the Lord in the hopes that my poetry would aid in their search. I also hope that these poems assist those who are searching for hope and faith during a crisis. Some other poems in this book are the result of my own searching during difficult times in my life.

At times, I use metaphors that I hope will help others to relate to the message of faith and hope in the Lord that I am trying to convey.

I have included at least one Bible verse at the end of each poem to reference the main message I was reaching for. For those not familiar with the Bible, these pages are titled "From God's Own Word." All Scripture quotations except for one verse (which is marked "KJV") are taken from *The Life Application Study Bible, New International Version,* published by Tyndale House Publishers, Inc., and Zondervan Publishing House. Copyright © 1995 by Tyndale House Publishers, Inc., Wheaton, IL. There is space on each of these pages to record any of your own reflections.

I pray that if you know the Lord and have a deep, lasting relationship with Him, you will appreciate my humble words.

I pray that if maybe you have gotten caught up in earthly life, as we all do at times, and have sort of slacked on your commitment to Him, you will remember your God and renew your commitment.

I pray that if you do not know the Lord yet, you will find something here that will inspire you to seek to know Him, His love, and His faithfulness.

I pray that no matter where you are in life, you will find a renewed sense of love for, hope and faith in, and appreciation for Jesus. I pray that you will realize that He is always with us, no matter if we are in the deepest of the depths or the highest of the highs.

Most of all, I pray that God will be praised, honored, and glorified through the words in this book. If it were not for Him, none of these words would have been possible.

Dedication

All the Glory to God

To Him who loves us and has freed us from our sins,
To Him who paid our debt with His blood and earthly skin.
I pray that I might serve others in presenting His case;
May all the glory be Yours, God, as I humbly reveal Your grace.

"Each one should use whatever gift he has received
to serve others, faithfully administering God's
grace in its various forms" (1 Peter 4:10).

"To Him who loves us and has freed us from our sins
by His blood, and has made us a kingdom and priests to
serve His God and Father—to Him be glory and power
forever and ever! Amen" (Revelation 1:5–6).

Blessing

Blessed is the one who reads these prophetic words,
For they are His who has the double-edged sword.
Blessed are those who take to heart and hear;
Blessed are they—because the time is near.

These divine words are true. They won't deceive.
They have been written so that you may believe
That Jesus is the Christ and is God's only Son,
And that you may have life through God's Holy One.

Blessed are they who believe that God so loved each of us,
He sent His one and only Son, Jesus,
To save our souls through His death and His anguish—
That whoever believes in Him shall not perish.

From God's Own Word

"Blessed is the one who reads the words of this prophecy, and blessed are those who hear it and take to heart what is written in it, because the time is near" (Revelation 1:3).

"These words are trustworthy and true" (Revelation 22:6).

"But these are written that you may believe that Jesus is the Christ, the Son of God, and that believing you may have life in His name" (John 20:31).

Section One

The Truest Story
Ever Lived

Creation

In the beginning, God created the Earth.
To the heavens He also gave birth.
God said, "Let there be light," and there was light.
God called the light "day" and the darkness "night."

God separated water from water with the sky
And said, "Let there be ground appear that is dry."
To mark day from night, He made two great lights,
One to rule the day, and one to rule the night.

He also made stars to give light to the earth.
There was night and day, and God saw their great worth.
God said, "Let there be living creatures, and let birds fly
Above the earth, across the expanse of the sky."

So God created each and every living thing,
Those that live in water and those that fly with wing.
And He said, "Let there be creatures to roam the lands."
So all of the animals were made with God's hands.

Then God said, "In our image, let us make man."
So God created both—the man and the woman.
Then the Lord planted a garden in the east,
With trees that grew food that was fit for a feast.

Also in the garden was the Tree of Life,
And the Tree of Knowledge of good and of strife.
Thus they were complete, the heavens and the earth,
And to every living thing, God had given birth.

From God's Own Word

"In the beginning God created the heavens
and the earth" (Genesis 1:1).

"And God saw that it was good" (Genesis 1:24).

"Then God said, 'Let us make man in our
image, in our likeness'" (Genesis 1:26).

Sin

Then the Lord commanded the man, "You are free
To eat in this garden from any tree.
But don't eat from the Tree of Good and Evil,
For you will surely die and cause upheaval."

But the Serpent told the woman, "You will not die,
For God knows if you eat of it, it will open your eye."
She saw the fruit was good for gaining wisdom and insight
And could not resist the temptation to take a bite.

She took some, ate it, and then gave some to the man.
Then their eyes were opened, and this is when sin began.
Then the Lord God called to the man, "Where are you?"
He answered, "I was naked, so I hid from your view."

God asked the man, "Have you eaten from the tree?
Have you taken what I commanded was not free?"
The man pointed to the woman for all the blame.
The woman said that it was to the Serpent's shame.

The Lord God punished each of them with a curse.
From now on, each of their lives would be much worse.
The Lord made garments of skin for Adam and his wife.
But, they could no longer eat from the Tree of Life.

They were not allowed to freely reach out their hand
But now had to grow their own food on cursed land.
Therefore, sin entered the world through one man.
Still, God would provide a covering through His plan.

When the Lord saw humanity's evil ways, He was filled with pain.
He said, "I will wipe out humankind. I will send a drowning rain."
But since He is slow to anger and abounding in love,
He offers forgiveness for our sin from above.

Just as God covered the sin of Adam and Eve,
He offers us forgiveness if we believe
That our sins are covered by the blood of Jesus
And that His reason for living was to die for us.

From God's Own Word

And the Lord God commanded the man, "You are free
to eat from any tree in the garden; but you must not eat
from the tree of the knowledge of good and evil, for when
you eat of it you will surely die" (Genesis 2:16–17).

"But the Lord God called to the man, 'Where are you'" (Genesis 3:9)?

"The Lord God made garments of skin for Adam and
his wife and clothed them" (Genesis 3:21).

Israel

Now, by faith, Abram, though he did not understand,
Left his country, people, his father's household, and land
When God said: I'll make you a great nation. I will bless you.
All the peoples on earth will be blessed through you.

God said: I will bless those who bless your great name,
And whoever curses you, I will put to shame.
Your offspring will be in a land where they'll be a stranger.
For four hundred years, they'll be abused and live in danger.

But I make this promise to you: With my mighty hand,
I will give you eternal possession of this land.
I will punish the nation they serve as slaves.
They will be repaid with eternal fiery graves.

So, it was by faith—though he did not understand—
That Abram obeyed God and left for a foreign land.
The Israelites were fruitful and filled the land,
But the Egyptians enslaved them with an oppressive hand.

The Lord had seen their misery and heard every tear,
So He came down and rescued them from pain and fear.
Then God asked them to celebrate on a certain day
As a reminder of how God delivered them this way.

He asked them to take a lamb or goat without defect,
Then take some blood from this sacrifice that was perfect.
He said that they should put it on the tops and sides of the doorjambs
Of all the houses where they would eat these perfect lambs.

God said: When I pass through to bring judgment on this town
And see the blood, I will pass over; I won't strike you down.
For generations to come, you shall observe this day.
You are to honor the Lord in this very special way."

The people had lived in Egypt for four hundred and thirty years
When the Lord God redeemed them from all their tears.
By faith, Moses kept the Passover and sprinkling of blood;
By faith, Noah believed God when He told him of the flood.

These men believed and obeyed God when they did not understand
How the Lord would lead them to an unseen Promised Land.
Faith is being sure of what we hope for but do not see;
It's being certain of God's promises to you and me.

From God's Own Word

"The Lord said to Abram, 'Leave your country, your people and your father's household and go to the land I will show you. I will make you a great nation and I will bless you'" (Genesis 12:1–2).

"The animals you choose must be year-old males without defect" (Exodus 12:5).

"Then they are to take some of the blood and put it on the sides and tops of the doorframes of the houses where they eat the lambs" (Exodus 12:7).

"The blood will be a sign for you on the houses where you are; and when I see the blood, I will pass over you" (Exodus 12:13).

Birth

This is what the Lord declares: "The days are coming
When I will raise up to David a righteous king.
He will reign wisely and do what is just and right."
To the darkness in this world, He will be a light.

And He'll be like no other; He will be divine.
Therefore, the Lord Himself will give you a sign:
The virgin will be with child and give birth to a son.
Immanuel will be the name of this Holy One.

When the time fully comes, God will send His Son,
Born of a woman and under law to redeem the sons.
Because we are sons, God delivers us from our graves.
He has made us heirs, so we are no longer slaves.

In those days, Caesar Augustus issued a decree,
So Joseph went up from a town in Galilee.
While he and his wife were there, the time came for the Son's birth.
Our divine Savior had been born a man here on Earth.

The shepherds were keeping watch over their flocks at night.
An angel appeared, and the glory of the Lord shone bright.
When the shepherds saw the angel, they were terrified.
But the angel said, Do not be afraid; I bring a good tide.

I bring for all the people good news of great joy.
Today, in a manger, was born a baby boy.
You will find Him wrapped in cloths. He is Christ our King.
Then the divine host appeared, praising God and saying:

"Glory to almighty God in the highest.
On earth, peace to men on whom His favor rests."
Jesus grew in stature, wisdom, and insight—
And in favor with God and mankind—until the time was right.

And so it was exactly as God had foresworn,
"Today in the town of David a Savior has been born."
The shepherds' fear turned to joy as the angels announced His birth.
They ran to see the baby, and then spread the news across the earth.

The greatest event in history had just taken place,
Just as God had promised—He sent to the world His grace.
If we're wise like the shepherds, we will daily seek the Lord
And spread the news across the earth that He's praised and adored.

From God's Own Word

"All this took place to fulfill what the Lord had said
through the prophet: 'The virgin will be with child and
will give birth to a son, and they will call Him Immanuel—
which means, "God with us"'" (Matthew 1:22–23).

"But the angel said to them, 'Do not be afraid. I bring you good news
of great joy that will be for all people. Today in the town of David a
Savior has been born to you; He is Christ the Lord'" (Luke 2:10–11).

Ministry

Jesus went up to the Jordan for John to baptize,
Not because He'd done any wrong in His Father's eyes.
But this was to fulfill what God had foretold,
Way back in the days of the ancients of old.

When He came out of the water, He saw up above
The Holy Spirit descend on Him like a dove.
A voice from heaven spoke words much like these:
"You are My Son, whom I love; with you I am pleased."

This was the start of the ministry of Jesus.
He was sent to preach good news and to teach us
How to find salvation and how we should live.
He was sent to deliver us from sin and forgive.

Jesus has told us, "I am the bread of life."
He also said, "I am the light of the world, the light of life.
I am the gate: Those who enter through me, I will save.
I am the resurrection and life, raised from the grave."

Jesus said, "I am the way and the truth and the life.
Do not let your hearts be troubled by this world's strife.
Trust in God; trust also in Me. I'll come and take you
To be with Me. I would not say this if it weren't true.

"All this I have spoken while still with you, but, in My name,
The Father will send the Holy Spirit to teach you the same.
He will remind you of everything I have said to you,
Peace I leave with you; my peace I give you."

Even as a young boy, Jesus had knowledge of God's plan—
That He would have to suffer for the redemption of man.
He was to die for the sins of the world and then rise from the dead
To fulfill His Father's will according to what He had said.

While here in this earthly region, Jesus was a preacher,
Yet He was so much more than just a "good teacher."
He was the Son of God, sent to save the human race
And preach the good news of salvation through God's grace.

Jesus did many wonders and other miraculous signs.
Many are not written in the book. 'Twas inspired, divine.
But these are written so that you may believe
That Jesus is the Christ, and life you may receive.

From God's Own Word

"When all the people were being baptized, Jesus was baptized too. And as He was praying, heaven was opened and the Holy Spirit descended on Him in bodily form like a dove. And a voice came from heaven: 'You are My Son, whom I love; with you I am well pleased'" (Luke 3:21–22).

"When Jesus spoke again to the people, He said, 'I am the light of the world. Whoever follows Me will never walk in darkness, but will have the light of life'" (John 8:12).

"I am the way and the truth and the life. No one comes to the Father except through Me" (John 14:6).

Passover/Trial

Now, there came the day for the Lamb to be a sacrifice—
A Lamb without blemish or defect to pay the price.
It was the Passover, the day of unleavened bread,
The day to honor God according to what He said.

When the hour came for the Supper of Last,
Jesus sent His apostles to arrange the repast.
He sent Peter and John, saying, "Go and prepare
For us to eat the Passover, the last meal we'll share."

Then Jesus and His apostles reclined at the table.
He said, "I have eagerly desired to be able
To eat this Passover with you before My pain,
For I tell you I will not eat it again.

"I will not eat it again until it is fulfilled
In the kingdom of God, what the Father has willed.
The Lamb of God will shed His blood as a sacrifice,
To save His people from sin—His blood will suffice."

On the night the Lord was betrayed, He took bread,
And when He had given thanks, He broke it and said,
"This is My body, which is for you; remember Me."
In the same way, with the cup, He said, "Remember Me."

"In My blood, this cup is the new promise.
Remember Me when you drink from this chalice.
For whenever you eat this bread and drink this cup,
You remember your deliverance—when I was lifted up."

Then Jesus went to Gethsemane with all His men.
"Sit here while I go over there and pray," He said to them.
He found them sleeping when He returned from prayer.
He said, "Rise, let us go! Here comes My betrayer!"

Now the betrayer had arranged a signal with some men.
He told them, "The one I kiss is the man. Arrest Him."
At once, Judas kissed Him while His men watched in awe,
Then they took Him to the high priest and the teachers of the law.

Pilate found no reason for Jesus to be crucified,
But "Crucify! Crucify!" is what the people cried.
Pilate had Jesus flogged. His soldiers placed on His head
A crown of thorns, and. "Hail, king of the Jews," they said.

From God's Own Word

"And He took bread, gave thanks and broke it, and gave it to them, saying, 'This is my body given for you; do this in remembrance of me.' In the same way, after the supper He took the cup, saying, 'This cup is the new covenant in my blood, which is poured out for you'" (Luke 22:19–20).

"The men seized Jesus and arrested Him" (Mark 14:46).

"They took Jesus to the high priest, and all the chief priests, elders and teachers of the law came together" (Mark 14:53).

"As soon as the chief priests and their officials saw Him, they shouted, 'Crucify! Crucify'" (John 19:6)!

Crucifixion

Pilate had willfully handed Jesus over to die,
Even though he had found no legal reason why.
There were two other men to be led out to the place.
Only two were guilty. Jesus had no sins or disgrace.

They divided up His clothes by casting lots.
They had fulfilled prophecy through their evil plots.
When He asked the Father to forgive them for what they do,
He opened the way of salvation for me and you.

From the sixth hour till the ninth, darkness covered the land.
When He said, "Father, I commit my spirit into your hands,"
Right then, the curtain of the temple was torn in two.
Christ's death opened the door to God for me and you.

At the moment when the curtain of the temple was torn,
Many people who had died were raised to life, reborn.
They came out of their tombs and to many would appear.
Those who were guarding Jesus were overcome with fear.

"Surely He was the Son of God!" they exclaimed.
Because of their unbelief, they were afraid and ashamed.
They had been in the presence of God's holy Son
But refused to believe He was the promised Holy One.

Don't wait too long to believe in Christ Jesus,
To repent and thank Him for dying for us.
"Get rid of the old that you may be new" (Paul's advice),
For Christ, our Passover Lamb, has been sacrificed.

He was pierced for our sins; by God His fate was sealed.
Our punishment was on Him; by His wounds we are healed.
We are not redeemed with any perishable thing,
But with the precious blood of Christ, the Lamb's suffering.

Jesus was nailed to a cross. He was crucified.
Through His most precious blood, we are justified.
Whoever believes in Him is not condemned,
But whoever does not believe is already condemned.

From God's Own Word

"At that moment the curtain of the temple was torn
in two from top to bottom" (Matthew 27:51).

"For you know that it was not with perishable things such as silver
and gold that you were redeemed from the empty way of life handed
down to you from your forefathers, but with the precious blood
of Christ, a lamb without blemish or defect" (1 Peter 1:18–19).

Resurrection/Ascension

As evening approached, there came Joseph, a rich man.
He wanted to bury Christ before the Sabbath began.
So he asked Pilate if he could take the body down,
To bury it in a tomb, in a garden, in the same town.

With Pilate's permission, they took the body away.
Nicodemus was also there to help on that day.
They wrapped the body in strips of linen and spice,
Then placed it in a tomb that would easily suffice.

Joseph rolled a stone in front of the tomb then went away.
Two of the women sat across from the tomb on that day.
They saw where the tomb was—where the Lord was laid
After His crucifixion, after the world's debt was paid.

The next day, the chief priests went to Pilate and said,
"We're afraid His men will say that He rose from the dead."
So Pilate put a seal on the tomb and then placed a guard
To make certain that an exit was impossibly hard.

The women took spices on the first day of the week.
They found the tomb, but not what they came to seek.
The body of the Lord was gone—it seemed to disappear.
Then, suddenly, two men—in clothes like lightning—appeared.

In their fright, the women bowed down, The men said,
"Why do you look for the living among the dead?
He is not here; He has risen. Come see where He lay."
It is just as He said; He was raised on the third day.

Christ is the first fruits of those who have fallen asleep.
The day of salvation has come for those who weep.
For, since death came through Adam, the fall of a man,
The resurrection of the dead comes also through one Man.

Jesus said, "All authority has been given to me."
Therefore, go and make disciples in every country,
Baptizing them in the name of the Father, and of the Son,
And of the Holy Spirit. These holy three are one.

When Jesus came to His disciples, He said to them,
"You will receive power and witness in Jerusalem."
After He said this, He was taken up before their eyes.
A cloud hid Him from their sight while they looked to the skies.

As they were looking intently up into the sky,
Two angels stood beside them and asked them, "Why?
Why do you stand here looking into the sky that way?
This same Jesus will come back in this same way someday."

From God's Own Word

"In their fright the women bowed down with their faces to the ground, but the men said to them, 'Why do you look for the living among the dead? He is not here; He has risen'"!
(Luke 24:5-6)

"After the Lord Jesus had spoken to them, He was taken up into heaven and He sat at the right hand of God" (Mark 16:19).

Church

They were all together when the day of Pentecost came.
They heard sounds like strong wind, and they saw tongues of flames.
The tongues separated, and on each of them came to rest.
They were all filled with the Holy Spirit; each one was blessed.

Now, there were many God-fearing Jews there, old and young,
And the Spirit empowered them to hear in other tongues.
They were in Jerusalem; they were there from every land.
A crowd came because what they heard, they could understand.

Utterly amazed, they asked, How can this be?
Are not all these men who are speaking from Galilee?
How is it that each of us hears them in his own tongue?
We can hear them proclaiming God in our own tongues.

Amazed and perplexed, they asked one another,
What does this mean, that we can all understand each other?
Some people, however, made fun of them and said,
They have had too much wine and it has gone to their head.

Then Peter said, "These men have not had too much wine,"
For it was early in the morning. Why, it was only nine!
Listen, this man Jesus was accredited to you
By God with miracles, wonders, and signs, too.

This Man was handed over with an immeasurable cost,
For He was put to death by being nailed to a cross.
But God raised Him from the dead on the third day,
Freeing Him from the agony of death and decay.

God raised Jesus to life, and we are all His witness.
Therefore, let all of Israel be assured and profess:
God has made Jesus, who was crucified, Lord and Christ.
Because of God's love for us, His Son was sacrificed.

You must repent and be baptized, every one of you,
In the name of Jesus Christ for your soul to be made new.
In view of God's mercy, offer yourselves to Him
As an act of worship for removing all your sin.

From God's Own Word

"God raised this Jesus to life, and we are all witnesses to the fact. Exalted to the right hand of God, He has received from the Father the promised Holy Spirit and has poured out what you now see and hear" (Acts 2:33).

"Repent and be baptized, every one of you, in the name of Jesus Christ for the forgiveness of your sins. And you will receive the gift of the Holy Spirit" (Acts 2:38).

Second Coming/Heaven

Brothers, don't worry about those who have fallen asleep,

And don't grieve like those who have no hope, who can only weep.

For since we believe that Jesus died and rose again,

We believe the dead in Christ will be raised also then.

For the Lord will come down from heaven with a loud command,

With the voice of the angel and a trumpet call so grand.

The dead in Christ will rise first. Then, those who are still here

Will be caught up together in the air when He appears.

We will be together forever with our Lord Jesus.

Therefore, encourage each other with His promise to us.

And about the times and dates we do not need to write,

The day of the Lord will come as a thief in the night.

This story began with God's giving everything its birth,

And it ends with His promise of a new heaven and Earth.

It began with man's sin. Death came through weakness—the great fall.

But through God's Son comes redemption, eternal life for all.

John saw the new heaven and Earth (the first had passed away),

And he heard a loud voice from the throne of God say:

Now the dwelling of God is with men. He will live with them.

They will be His people; God Himself will be with men.

He will forever wipe away the tears from their eyes.

There will be no more death, mourning, or painful cries.

For the old order of things will surely pass away

When the Lord comes back as promised on that day.

John also saw the water of the River of Life.

On each side of the river stood the Tree of Life.

Bearing twelve crops of fruit, each month its fruit would yield,

And through the leaves of the tree, every nation is healed.

The throne of God and the Lamb will be in the city.

His servants will serve Him. On their foreheads His name will be.

They will see His face, and there will be no more night.

They won't need a lamp or sun, for the Lord will give them light.

He who was on the throne said, "I will make everything new.

Write this down, for these words are trustworthy and true.

Behold, I am coming soon. Blessed is he who keeps My word."

And so we will be forever with Christ Jesus our Lord. Amen.

From God's Own Word

"Then I saw a new heaven and a new earth, for the first heaven and the first earth had passed away" (Revelation 21:1).

I heard a loud voice from the throne saying, "Now the dwelling of God is with men, and He will live with them. They will be His people, and God Himself will be with them and be their God. He will wipe every tear from their eyes. There will be no more death or mourning or crying or pain, for the old order of things has passed away." He who was seated on the throne said, "I am making everything new! Then He said, "Write this down, for these words are trustworthy and true." (Revelation 21:3–5)

Invitation

Once, Paul and Silas were going to the place of prayer.
They were met by a slave girl while on their way there.
She foretold the future and made money for her owners.
She made her predictions through a spirit that had *known* her.

Paul became very troubled by the way that she behaved.
She kept shouting, "These men are telling you how to be saved."
It was not the message that bothered the men so much,
But rather it was the spirit that had her in its clutch.

Finally, Paul became so troubled that he turned around
And told the spirit, "In the name of Jesus, you are bound."
At that moment, the spirit left her; it was made to flee.
The owners were mad because the girl had been set free.

The owners realized their hope for making money was lost,
So they captured Paul and Silas to make them pay the cost.
Paul and Silas were beaten and flogged and then thrown into jail,
But it would not take too long for justice to prevail.

About midnight, Paul and Silas were praying and singing.
Suddenly, there was an earthquake. Cell doors were swinging.
Everyone's chains came loose; the guard awoke and was afraid.
He drew his sword and was about to kill himself with its blade.

But Paul shouted, "Don't harm yourself! We are all here!"
The jailer called for lights, rushed in, and fell, trembling in fear.
He brought them out and asked, "Sirs, what must I do to be saved?"
They replied, "Believe in the Lord Jesus and you will be saved."

This promise is for you and your entire household.
When they spoke God's Word to them, they believed what they were told.
The jailer took them and washed their wounds, although it was late.
Then, he and all his household were baptized; they did not wait.

The jailer brought the two into his house and served them a meal.
He was filled with joy because his own wounds had been healed.
He had come to believe in God, he and his whole clan.
Each one put their trust in Jesus and were saved through God's plan.

How about you? Do you believe God's truth today?
Have you asked Jesus to save you from death and decay?
For to all who receive Him, to those who believe in His name,
He gives the right to become children of God—without shame.

We are therefore buried with Him through baptism into death.
Just as He was raised from the dead, we, too, will have new breath.
The Spirit and the Bride say, "Come!" And let him who hears say,
"Come!" Whoever is thirsty, let him come and drink today.

From God's Own Word

"Sirs, what must I do to be saved?" They replied, "Believe in the Lord Jesus, and you will be saved—you and your household." Then they spoke the word of the Lord to him and to all the others in his house. At that hour of the night the jailer took them and washed their wounds; then immediately he and all his family were baptized. The jailer brought them into his house and set a meal before them; he was filled with joy because he had come to believe in God—he and his whole family." (Acts 16:30–34)

Salvation

Page by page, we read how the truest story has unfurled.
We read how through one man, death came into this world.
How God's heart was saddened with the choices made by man.
But, because of His love, He offered a grace-filled plan.

He had a plan for forgiveness right from the beginning.
He promised to send a Savior that would be a great king.
He would send His only begotten Son to the Earth
To renew and restore humankind with spiritual rebirth.

He knew from the start that there would be doubters and naysayers,
Those whose feet would be entangled in the Devil's snares.
Because of their disbelief and refusal to repent,
They will suffer forever in the place of torment.

He also knew about those who *would* believe in His Son,
Those who would believe His promise to send this Holy One.
Even though they cannot see, nor can they understand,
Through faith and trust they follow God into the Promised Land.

Just as God covered Adam and Eve's shame with a ram's skin,
He will cover our shame with divine blood and human skin.
The only thing we can do to be covered by God's grace
Is believe that Jesus died in our most sinful place.

I pray that my humble version of the truest story
Will help others to believe and give to God all the glory.
Are you a believer in Jesus or in the betrayer?
If you believe in Jesus, say something like this prayer:

"Father God, I believe that Jesus is Your holy Son.
He is the Savior of the world; He is the Promised One.
I believe that He died to pay for my sins, my discord, and my strife.
And after three days, He rose again to eternal life.

"I confess to you that I am a sinner, and I pray
That You will forgive me and save me from death and decay.
Please welcome me into Your kingdom as a citizen.
I ask in the precious name of Jesus. Thank you. Amen."

Don't wait too long to ask Jesus to make your wrongs right,
For the day of the Lord will come as a thief in the night.
And after His hand closes the salvation door,
Your chance for endless life *with Him* will be lost forevermore.

From God's Own Word

"And this is the testimony: God has given us eternal life, and this life is in His Son. He who has the Son has life; he who does not have the Son of God does not have life" (1 John 5:11–12).

"Stop doubting and believe" (John 20:27).

Section Two

Salvation

Salvation

Salvation is not something we can earn.
It's only available to those who will turn
Their hearts toward Jesus and believe in Him—
That when He died, He paid for all of their sin.

Salvation is not a result of our deeds.
It's impossible to grow by planting seeds.
We can't buy salvation with any amount.
Only the grace of God can clear our account.

It's not because of any rite we've received
Or any honors from mankind that we achieve.
It's not because we go to a certain church.
It's only if we go in our hearts and search.

If we just have faith in this promise of His,
Then all our debts He will gracefully dismiss.
Salvation is free for all who believe
That eternal life is the gift they receive.

Thank you, Lord Jesus, for your free gift of grace
That saved my wretched soul from the other place.
And O my heart, You really did overwhelm
So that I could live in Your heavenly realm.

From God's Own Word

"For it is by grace you have been saved, through faith—
and this is not from yourselves, it is the gift of God—not
by works, so that no one can boast" (Ephesians 2:8–9).

Lifted Up

The Israelites had traveled from Mount Hor to the Red Sea,
But the people grew impatient for what they could not see.
They'd forgot the miracles that God had already done,
Providing them with food and water when they had none.

They spoke out against God and Moses when they said,
"Why have you brought us where there is no water or bread?"
They also said, "We detest this miserable food!"
God soon became angry with their ungrateful mood.

So the Lord sent venomous snakes among them;
They bit many people—all those He was to condemn.
The people came to Moses and asked if he would pray
That God would forgive them and take the snakes away!

The Lord said: Make a snake and put it on a pole.
Then, those who believe with all their heart and soul
Will be saved when they look at the pole and believe.
Their wounds will be healed. Life is what they'll receive.

So Moses made a bronze snake and put in on a pole.
Those who looked and believed were once again made whole.
It was not the bronze snake that healed their deadly bite,
But their belief that God had the power and the might.

Like those bitten, doomed to die from the venom within,
We are condemned to die from the poison of our sin.
We must believe like those who asked Moses to pray.
We must ask Jesus to forgive us and take our sins away.

When we need physical healing, we look for the sign.
We look for the pole with the serpents that are entwined.
When we need spiritual healing, we should look to Him
Who was lifted up on the cross to pay for our sin.

The snake was lifted as a sign of the coming day,
When the Son of Man would be lifted in the same way,
So that *all who believe* in Him may *have* eternal life,
For God so loved us that He gave His only Son's life.

From God's Own Word

"Just as Moses lifted up the snake in the desert, so the Son of Man must be lifted up, that everyone who believes in Him may have eternal life. For God so loved the world that He gave His one and only Son, that whoever believes in Him shall not perish but have eternal life" (John 3:14–16).

Repent and Be Baptized

Jesus came to the Jordan for John to baptize.
When He came out of the water, He saw with His eyes
The Spirit of God descend on Him like a dove.
Then God said,
"You are My Son in whom I'm well pleased and love."

He did not get baptized to wash away any sin.
It was to respect the Father—to obey Him—
And to mark the start of His work as a minister,
For He had never sinned or done anything sinister.

Christ set an example for us to follow,
To show us how our sins can be made white as snow.
We must repent and be baptized—we have to believe.
Then, the Spirit of God is the gift we will receive.

Jesus is the only Man ever to live on Earth
To be sinless and born by virgin birth.
Salvation can only be found through faith in Him.
He is God's Holy One, completely without sin.

Unlike Jesus, we are guilty of wicked deeds.
He will forgive us and provide for all our needs.
But first, we must repent and be baptized in His name,
The Father, Son, and Holy Spirit—one and the same.

From God's Own Word

"Repent and be baptized, every one of you, in the name of Jesus Christ for the forgiveness of your sins. And you will receive the gift of the Holy Spirit" (Acts 2:38).

The Bridge

He was nailed to a cross to prove His worth.
He was suspended between heaven and earth.
Most of the people on earth had rejected Him,
And God in heaven would not yet receive Him.

He was betrayed with a kiss; that was the plot.
They divided His garments by casting lots.
They placed on His head a crown made of thorns.
The people and rulers would only mock and scorn.

There was a sign above Him announcing the news:
It said, "This is the king of the Jews."
They pierced His heart with an unyielding sword.
All of this was done to fulfill the Lord's Word.

If He wanted, He could have come down at any time,
But then I would be guilty of these sins of mine.
The cross on which He died now forms a bridge
That connects us to heaven. What a privilege!

He was guilty of nothing yet was crucified.
A perfect Lamb for our sins God did provide.
Thank you, Lord Jesus, for your suffering
And for your sweet salvation that it did bring.

From God's Own Word

"In Him and through faith in Him we may approach God
with freedom and confidence" (Ephesians 3:12).

"Father, forgive them, for they know not
what they are doing" (Luke 23:34).

"I tell you the truth, today you will be with
me in paradise" (Luke 23:43).

[Speaking to John and Mary, Jesus said,]
"Dear woman, here is your son...
Here is your mother" (John 19:26,27).

"My God, my God, why have You forsaken me" (Matthew 27:46)?

"I am thirsty" (John 19:28).

"It is finished" (John 19:30).

"Father, into Your hands I commit My Spirit" (Luke 23:46).

W CROSS RDS

"Father, forgive them, for they know not what they do."
It is out of ignorance that they mock you.
They did not seek you, or else they would have known
The kind of mercy that you have shown.

"I tell you the truth, today you will be
With Me in paradise." Truly you'll see
The gates of heaven. Because you believe,
I am the payment that your debts receive.

"Here is your mother... Dear woman, here is your son,"
He said to Mary and John - the latter being the Loved One.
When He asked them to take care of each other,
He was teaching us how to love one another.

"My God, my God, why have You forsaken Me?"
Did He really believe that God could not see
All that they were doing to Christ our Lord?
No, He was fulfilling what God said in His Word.

"I am thirsty," said Jesus. It was complete,
With nails through His hands and also His feet.
The price was paid in full; there's nothing else to do
But believe that His anguish was for me and you.

"It is finished," is what Christ Jesus said,
Just before He bowed His thorn-crowned head.
There is nothing we can add to, or take away from,
What Christ did on the cross that day.

"Father, I commit My Spirit into Your hands."
Then darkness came over the entire land,
And the curtain of the temple was torn in two,
Which opened the way to God for me and you.

Cross-Eyed

There are some who say they don't believe it's true
That Christ really died on that cross for me and you.
It's much too hard for them ever to comprehend
That the *Son of God* would want to be their friend.

They ask, "Why would He care if we died in our own sin?
Why does it matter to Him whether we lose or win?
Why would a stranger want to die for our wicked deeds,
And why does He care about providing for our needs?"

They can't believe He endured suffering on the cross
So that He could offer salvation without any cost.
They say, "Why would He have done that for us?
What is the true motive of this Man called Jesus?"

Christ died for us while we were in the midst of sin.
Because of God's love, we are reconciled through Him.
The power that raised Him from His holy grave
Is the same power by which He's able to save.

In this world of sin, as we struggle and fight,
We can have this power if we keep Him in our sight.
If we keep our eyes fixed on Him each and every day,
Then one day we will see and be able to say,

"I could see a crown of thorns upon His precious head;
A ray of light revealed each drop of blood that was shed.
With my eye, I could see the cross on which He died.
I suppose some could say that my vision is *cross-eyed.*"

From God's Own Word

"Greater love has no one than this: that he lay
down his life for his friends" (John 15:13).

"But God demonstrates His own love for us in this: While
we were still sinners, Christ died for us" (Romans 5:8).

So Loved

I once looked up into the gray winter sky.
There was a man up there who made me cry
Because He had nails through His hands and feet.
A crown of thorns;, His flesh was torn and beat.

As my gaze met His, and without a word,
I knew He was the Christ of whom I'd heard.
So, speaking with my heart, I asked Him why
Did He do this thing that had made me cry.

His Spirit replied, I love you my child.
It was to cleanse that which had been defiled.
The wages of sin are death and its sting,
But life and victory are what My cross bring.

"Nailed to a cross" with my soul to defend.
His kind of love—I just can't comprehend.
That God so loved me.... He gave His only Son.
My debt has been paid by God's Holy One!

God raised Him from the dead on the third day.
All those who believe are saved from decay.
Thanks be to God for our Lord Jesus
And the victory over death He gives us!

From God's Own Word

"For God so loved the world that He gave His one
and only Son that whoever believes in Him shall
not perish but have eternal life" (John 3:16).

"'Where, O death, is your victory? Where, O death, is your
sting?' The sting of death is sin, and the power of sin is the
law. But thanks be to God! He gives us the victory through
our Lord Jesus Christ" (1 Corinthians 15:55–56).

His Story

He is called Lord Jesus, Christ the King, and this is His story:
He came to change His crown of thorns into a crown of glory.
The Spirit of the Lord is on Him. He has been anointed
To preach good news to the poor, to the broken, and disappointed.

He came to build a bridge made only of two boards and three nails,
To proclaim freedom for captives—to release them from their jails—
To declare recovery of sight for the spiritually blind,
To comfort those who mourn, all the broken hearts he came to bind.

He came to release the oppressed and to seek and save the lost,
To bestow the Lord's favor on them and to pay their sin's cost,
To bless with beauty, praise, and joy instead of despair and strife.
Those who persevere and love Him will receive the crown of life.

From God's Own Word

"The Spirit of the Sovereign Lord is on Me, because the Lord has anointed Me to preach good news to the poor. He has sent Me to bind up the brokenhearted, to proclaim freedom for the captives and release from darkness for the prisoners, to proclaim the year of the Lord's favor" (Isaiah 61:1–2).

At the Last Day

We often wonder what it will be like at the last day
When we are face-to-face with the Lord. What will we say?
More important than this is what *He* will say or do.
Will He say, "Well done, my child," or will He frown upon you?

Do you think that you will be happy to be by His side,
Or do you think that you'll wish you could run and hide?
Is there any way for us to ensure where we will go
When we leave this Earth? Is there any way we can know?

In God's own Word, He tells us His Son was sent to save,
That Jesus died to pay our debt so we won't see the grave,
That whoever believes in Him, He will not condemn,
But whoever does not believe already stands condemned.

"I am the resurrection and the life," Jesus said.
He who believes in Me will live; he will never be dead.
Even though his flesh and bones will vanish from this Earth,
His Spirit will live forever with spiritual rebirth.

No one can see God's kingdom unless they are born again.,
You must be born of God to become a citizen.
To all those who receive Christ, those who believe in His name,
He gives the right to be born of God—children without shame.

God has promised that we *all* will be raised from the dead,
Some to everlasting life, and some to torment and dread.
Do you believe that Jesus can save you from death and decay?
If you believe, ask Him to raise you up at the last day.

From God's Own Word

"I am the resurrection and the life. He who believes in Me will live, even though he dies; and whoever lives and believes in Me will never die. Do you believe this" (John 11:25–26)?

Precious Love

I saw a man on a cross.
He said that for us there is no cost,
Only to believe what He does say.
We should open our hearts to Him today.

If we just ask Him to come in,
He will quickly remove any sin.
In our hearts, He will open a door
To the place we will be forevermore.

To be with the Lord up above
In the presence of His precious love!
"Father, forgive them,
They know not what they do."
How precious, then,
Is His love for me and you?

Thank you, Lord, for your sacrifice,
And that, for my sins, You did suffice.
By the way, this Man's name is Jesus.
He says, "Do not fear." He is always with us.

From God's Own Word

For the wages of sin is death, but the gift of God
is eternal life in Christ Jesus our Lord"
(Romans 6:23).

The Lamb of God

The Lamb of God was slain
His **blood** was not in vain
His **blood** washes our stain
His **blood** comforts our pain
His **blood** falls like sweet rain
His **blood** was shed for our gain
His **blood** fills our hearts' domain
His **blood** is our atonement attain
His **blood** is our innocence regain
His **blood** in His kingdom's reign
His **blood** runs through our vein
His **blood** is our salvation obtain
His **blood** is our priestly ordain
His **blood** is our harvest grain
His **blood** is our faith remain
His **blood** is His love sustain
His **blood** unlocks our chain
His **blood** is our sin refrain
His **blood** for us was drain
His **blood** is evil's restrain
His **blood** was not in vain
The Lamb of God was slain

From God's Own Word

"Worthy is the Lamb, who was slain" (Revelation 5:12).

"They have washed their robes and made them
white in the blood of the Lamb"
(Revelation 7:14).

The Access Bridge

There once came a man with a mission to build a new bridge.

It was to span the widest of gaps on the highest ridge.

It had to stretch from Earth to eternity and be strong

So it could hold the weight of the world's decisions so wrong.

So with only two boards, three nails, and His pure flesh and blood,

He built a bridge strong and high so we'd be safe from any flood.

When we trust Him, there's nothing that
can knock us from this bridge,

Not death nor life, neither the deepest of
depth nor the highest ridge.

From God's Own Word

For I am convinced that neither death nor life, neither angels nor demons, neither present nor the future, nor any powers, neither height nor depth, nor anything else in all creation, will be able to separate us from the love of God that is in Christ Jesus our Lord. (Romans 8:38-39)

Time to Confess

If you have betrayed the Lord Jesus with a scoffing kiss,
If you have made a grave pact with the Devil, just know this:
Unlike Judas, the betrayer of God, you still have time
To ask the Lord to forgive you and wash away the grime.

But you must make your decision right away. Please, don't wait,
Lest you miss closing hell's door—and opening heaven's gate.
Take hold of God's promise, that if we believe in Jesus,
And if we confess our sins to Him, He will forgive us.

From God's Own Word

"For I will forgive their wickedness and remember their sins no more" (Hebrews 8:12).

Be Very Afraid

My sister once told me that she wanted to make it clear

That her God is a loving God of which she has no fear.

She said she believed God did not want her to be afraid,

As He would never cause her to be scared or dismayed.

While I knew exactly what Denise was trying to say,

I tried to explain that I meant *fear* in a different way.

I said, "Try to liken God to the parents that we've had.

Compare our Divine Father with our earthly mom and dad."

Our parents strived to warn us of the dangers here on Earth.

They used rules to guide and protect us since the day of our birth.

It's for safety and protection that parents have such rules.

They instill virtue and wisdom so we will not live as fools.

They had rules like these: Don't run with scissors in your hand,

And stay away from people who tempt you with contraband.

Also, don't play in the street; you could get hit by a car.

If you get lost, stop and wait for me, right where you are.

Now, if we look at these rules that our parents set for us
And compare them with the teachings of our Lord Christ Jesus,
We will see that these guidelines aren't to keep us from pleasure,
But are to keep us safe from harm. They are a key to treasure.

If we walk in His ways instead of doing whatever we please,
His guidance will protect us from all kinds of pain and disease.
But if you have ignored Him and have wandered from His ways,
Stop and wait for Him. He will seek the lost and bring back the strays.

Be very afraid of the power that God has to destroy,
Or you could be lost forever—in exchange for fleeting joy.
We must first realize God's power to grasp this kind of fear.
Respect the Lord and His guidance with the highest revere.

From God's Own Word

"The fear of the Lord is the beginning of knowledge, but fools despise wisdom and discipline" (Proverbs 1:7).

"The fear of the Lord is the key to this treasure" (Isaiah 33:6).

Bath Time

I heard a man tell a story of his adopting two Ethiopian boys.

This man wasn't sure that they could ever
share a family's kind of love or joys.

Their culture was just so different, and so was the color of their skin.

They didn't even speak the same language,
so how could a kinship begin?

Until meeting these boys, he didn't know that
dirt would show on skin so brown.

He thought it would sort of "blend in," that is,
until his world turned upside down.

His wife asked him to do something that forever
changed his sight and his scope.

She asked for his help in bathing one of the
boys. She handed him some soap.

"No," he pleaded, "that's not something I am
able to do. Please, don't make me."

She replied, "Pick which child you will
bathe," ignoring his desperate plea.

"But these children are filthy. They even
have bugs living in their hair,

And their odor is foul," he cried, before
deciding he would do his share.

As the child played in the stream of water,
this man watched him from behind.

He found mercy, a kind of love and compassion
that he was not prepared to find.

He described what he saw in the tub as he
formed four fingers into a frame.

As he began to speak, his voice cracked. Out
poured his humility and shame.

He said, "I saw what looked like a bag of
dirty black flesh filled with bones,

A head full of bugs, and a belly swelled up
with starving moans and groans.

I realized in that instant that's exactly what
God sees when he looks at us.

He sees our sin and darkness; all our thoughts
and actions are dirty and rebellious."

There was not a dry eye as he compared God's
ways with our human ways so vile,

Explaining how these keep us from God and
the only way we can reconcile.

Our dirt does not blend in. We cannot hide
our wicked and depraved deeds.

We have no hope of ever being cleansed
unless the Holy One intercedes.

Because our debt was paid with the blood
of Jesus when He was crucified,

We can rejoice in God through Him and be
washed whiter than snow—purified.

Whoever believes in God's Son, no matter how sinful and depraved,

And is baptized, is cleansed by His blood.
They have new life; they are saved.

From God's Own Word

"God the Father knew you and chose you long ago, and His Spirit made you holy. As a result, you have obeyed Him and have been cleansed by the blood of Jesus Christ" (1 Peter 1:2).

A Great Fish Story

There are people who think that Jonah's tale is just a great fish story.
They don't believe that the account could really be a part of history.
They believe it's a just parable about how God will reprimand
When we try to flee after we have disobeyed His command.

There are those who say they believe that it *is* a true story.
Others will tell you that it's just an interesting allegory.
Still more say, "It must be a fable, for it's much too grand.
It's a children's fairy tale that came straight from fairyland."

What do you say? Is it true, or is it just a great fish story?
Do you believe it's just a fairy tale or an allegory?
Can you believe God's Word even when you don't really understand
How a great fish can swallow a man and then spit him out on the sand?

I admit, to be in the belly of a fish is quite a story.
And sometimes I wonder what it would be like. Would it be gory?
But I, for one, believe—although I don't completely understand
That a fish swallowed a man and then vomited him onto dry land.

I believe in this miracle that brings to God all the glory.
If it weren't true, God's Word would say, "It's just a picture story."
If we try to say that a Bible story is just a tale that is grand,
We lose faith in His Word and become confused about His command.

Although I can't comprehend, I believe this tale is promissory.
Even when we've disobeyed and fled, we can again see God's glory.
Through this tale, we see how God can turn us around with a reprimand,
And that our salvation comes only from God, the Lord's righteous hand.

From God's Own Word

"In my distress I called to the Lord, and He answered me. From the depths of the grave I called for help, and You listened to my cry" (Jonah 2:1).

The Judgment Seat

There are some who say, "There's not really a hell."
To them, I would say, "Then we just might as well
Do what we please, with no concern for its evil,
For there'll be no punishment for causing upheaval."

And that would mean that we'd all go to the same place.
It won't matter to God, when we come face-to-face,
What we have done or what others have done to us.
Nothing will count when we look in the eyes of Jesus.

Does it seem logical that there'll be no consequence
For all the wrongdoing that just plain makes no sense,
That both good and evil will together reside
For all eternity - they will be - side by side?

For me, I believe what is written in God's Word,
That He gave the power to judge to Christ our Lord.
When the Son of Man comes with His heavenly glory,
He'll divide the people like in the Bible story.

He'll put the sheep on His right and the goats on His left.
Between believers and doubters, there'll be a great cleft.
He'll say to those on His right, "You are blessed; come with Me,"
And to those on His left, "You are cursed; depart from Me."

We must all appear before the judgment seat of Him,
Where we'll receive what's due for our righteousness and sin.
But for those who believe in what God's Word does say,
There'll be no condemnation on judgment day.

From God's Own Word

"He will put the sheep on His right and the goats on His left. Then the King will say to those on His right, 'Come, you who are blessed by My Father; take your inheritance, the kingdom prepared for you since the beginning of the world'" (Matthew 25:33–34).

"For we must all appear before the judgment seat of Christ, that each one may receive what is due him for the things done while in the body, whether good or bad" (2 Corinthians 5:10).

He Has Risen

"It is finished," said Jesus Christ our Lord,
To fulfill what God promised in His Word—
That He would send a Savior, a mighty King,
To pay our debt with His great suffering.

And when He cried out, He breathed His last.
All sins forgiven: present, future, and past.
For those who believe that He died for them,
Their debts were nailed to the cross with Him.

His body was taken down by two men,
Then wrapped with spices in strips of linen.
It was placed in a tomb cut out from rock.
A stone rolled in front was used as a lock.

On the first day of the week, at first light,
Some women went out to His burial site.
They went to anoint His body with spice,
Out of respect for His love and sacrifice.

When they arrived at the place He was laid,
An angel proclaimed, "Don't be afraid!
He is not here; He has risen!" He said,
"He is among the living, not the dead."

From God's Own Word

"Why do you look for the living among the dead?
He is not here; He has risen" (Luke 24:5–6)!

"Whoever believes and is baptized will be saved, but whoever
does not believe will be condemned" (Mark 16:16).

Translation

Whether a cross, a stake or a tree
Doesn't matter that much to me
The point of the story
That brings God the glory
Is that He died for you and me

Whether a cross, a stake or a tree
Doesn't matter that much to me
The result is the same
He took all our shame
When He died for you and me

Whether a cross, a stake or a tree
Doesn't matter that much to me
He took every sin
Away with him
When he died for you and me

Whether a cross, a stake or a tree
Doesn't matter that much to me
It's not on "what" he died
But it is "that" he died
When he died for you and me

Whether a cross, a stake or a tree
Doesn't matter that much to me
It's not on which piece of wood
But with His love, that He would
Die for you and me

Thank you, Lord Jesus.

From God's Own Word

"For what I received, I passed on to you as of first importance:
that Christ died for our sins according to the Scriptures,
that He was buried, and that He was raised on the third day
according to the Scriptures" (1 Corinthians 15:3–4).

He is the atoning sacrifice for our sins, and not only for ours
but also for the sins of the whole world.
1 John 2:2

Section Three

Why

Clay Pots

We have to remember when we're asking God why—
Why we all have flaws and why we have to cry,
Why must we fight battles that leaves us all with scars—
That some are broken, are crushed like glass jars.

We must keep in mind when pondering the turmoil
And the reasoning behind our struggles and toil
That the Lord patterns us with a distinct shape and form,
Because we each have a unique role to perform.

We are made of clay, and we're still being designed
By the Lord God for the purpose He has in mind.
We have no reason, no right to ask Him why,
For we can't see what we'll be when the clay is dry.

We're like clumps of wet clay in a skilled potter's hands
That will be made for its owner's needs and demands.
Some pots are made to carry water, large and small,
Some to hold food, plants, or flowers, short and tall.

Like the clay pots, at times we get damaged and hurt.
But we can grow nothing unless we have some dirt.
And without a source of water, tears for the soil,
There will be no harvest to show for all our toil.

So, we can't forget when we ask the Lord Jesus
Why we are like we are, why He made us like us,
That He has a purpose knows what we will be.
We must trust Him until we're able to see.

From God's Own Word

"Yet, O Lord, You are our Father. We are the clay, You are the Potter; we are all the work of Your hand" (Isaiah 64:8).

Why in the World?

Why does life sometimes seem so unfair?
Are there times when God just doesn't care?
Does He forget all about our justice
And just ignore those who do harm to us?
Has God lost the control He once had?
Has He lost His mind and just gone mad?
Does He have no power over this land?
Could He not help by just raising His hand?
Why is there so much anguish and pain,
Why death and war and waste-filled rain?
Some are lonely, hungry, and homeless;
Some are overwhelmed and feel hopeless.
Why isn't this life the way that we
Living here on Earth think it should be?
A life with peace, comfort, and pleasure,
A Paradise filled with divine treasure.
Where are the streets of gold which, we hear,
Are lined with the promise of "Not a tear,"
Where there's no evil, death, hate, or war?
Why are we so confused about where we are?

One reason for so much pain and heartache
Are the choices we humans sometimes make.
We live in a fallen world full of sin;
Freedom of choice is where sin does begin.
Have we forgotten about Eve and sin's birth,
The cause of this fallen world called Earth?
And we can't blame just Adam and Eve for the fall.
We're all guilty of sin, *one and all.*
But God did provide redemption for us
Through the death of His Son, Christ Jesus.
He knows we are human—weak against sin—
so He sent us a covering made of skin.
Like the ram that died to cover Eve's shame,
A perfect Lamb died to absolve us of blame.
Our hope for Paradise lies with the Lord
And in the faith to believe His mighty Word.
So for now, we must persevere with trust
And wait for the promise of the Lord Jesus,
That He will come and take us with Him
To Paradise, where there's not one hint of sin.

From God's Own Word

"So, do not throw away your confidence; it will be richly rewarded. You need to persevere so that when you have done the will of God, you will receive what He has promised" (Hebrews 10:35–36).

"He will wipe every tear from their eyes. There will be no more death or mourning or crying or pain" (Revelation 21:4).

Jars of Clay

Why do some people seem to suffer more than others?
One is born sickly but has healthy sisters and brothers.
Why does one person get through life without pain or illness,
While another can't have one day of good health, peace, or stillness?

Why does life for one person sometimes seem so unfair,
While another just glides right through it without a care?
One is born with a disease that lasts through their lifetime;
Another's life, from day one, seems completely sublime.

I guess there's just no way to know these answers right now.
We just have to trust God until He tells us why and how,
Even though, at times, it seems there will be no easy way
To explain all our suffering while we're in these jars of clay.

When we suffer with trials, distress, and all kinds of pain,
We must try to stay focused on our eternal gain.
We must fix our eyes not on what is seen but what is unseen,
For the unseen is eternal, and short-lived is the seen.

Do not lose heart, though outwardly we're wasting away,
Because inwardly we are being renewed day by day.
Our momentary troubles are achieving for us
An eternal glory that outweighs them all with Jesus.

We know that if this earthly tent we live in is destroyed,
We have a building from God to be forever enjoyed,
But only if we are reconciled to God through Jesus.
That's why God made Him who had no sin to be sin for us.

Why the Suffering?

Why are we often face-to-face with the ageless question of "Why?"

Why do bad things happen to good people? Why the tears we cry?

Why do we have struggles with the likes of war, racism, and hate?

Why so much illness and pain? Is death and sorrow our final fate?

Why must we suffer with all this hardship, disaster, and strife?

Why can't our happiness and comfort be
the sole purpose for our life?

Why are so many people hungry and
homeless, just plain down-and-out?

Why is there one problem after the other?
Why is there so much doubt?

Is this the payment for our wrongs? Are
these the rewards we have earned?

Have we already been tried and sentenced?,
Has the courtroom been adjourned?

Or could it be that we have just forgotten exactly where we are?

We're living in the fallen world where, at
times, things seem quite bizarre.

If God is all -good, why does He allow sin and evil to seem routine?

And if He is truly all-powerful, why doesn't He intervene?

Is He unable to put an end to all the cruel and wicked deeds,

Or is He just unwilling to stop evil and the pain that it breeds?

And do we dare complain to God about what appears to be bad for us

When we can't see the true intent of what
seems to be haphazardous?

How can we judge the right or wrong way
for the guiding wind to blow

When the final port to which our ship is
heading we don't even know?

To each one of us, God gave the freedom to make our own choice.

He gave us the right to either listen and learn or to ignore His voice.

It is our choice whether we let troubles
bring us down or make us strong.

It's our choice to trust God, that He has a fair
purpose for all that seems wrong.

There are many reasons why bad things
happen; one is the choices we make.

For sin entered the world through one man,
yet we're all guilty; make no mistake.

God is the Creator of the world. He is all-powerful and all good.

He will destroy sin and evil in His own
time; He promised that He would.

We can't see ahead to what winds will blow
our way. We only see the past.

When the winds blow brutally, ask God to
make you strong, firm, and steadfast.

Ask Him to give you a firm place to stand,
to set your feet upon a rock,

To use your trial as a lesson and a stepping-
stone, not a stumbling block.

Through what seemed to be the most horrid
day that Jesus would ever endure,

God brought forth salvation for the world.
Through Christ's pain we are made pure.

God and humankind are reconciled through
the suffering of His precious Son.

There's no other name under heaven by which
we can be saved. There is none.

If we choose to believe Jesus, that He paid
the debt we were supposed to pay,

We will see the beauty of His suffering when
He died on that Good Friday.

And if we believe that He rose from the dead,
we'll grasp His power to save.

He will bless us with His mercy and save us
from certain death and the grave.

From God's Own Word

"I have told you these things, so that in me you may have peace. In this world you will have trouble. But take heart! I have overcome the world" (John 16:33 NIV).

The Beauty of His Worst Day

We are often face-to-face with the ageless question of why.

Why do bad things happen to good people. Why the tears we cry?

Why do we have suffering and tragedy, disease and hate?

Why the pain and heartache? Just how much more can we tolerate?

If God is all good, why does He allow sins from the obscene?

And if He is all-powerful, why doesn't He intervene?

Is He *unable* to put an end to all the wicked deeds,

Or is He *unwilling* to stop evil and the pain it breeds?

Why must we struggle with all this hardship, disaster, and strife?

Isn't our happiness and comfort the whole purpose of life?

Is this payment for our wrongs? Is this the reward we have earned,

Or should we change our perspective and
call these lessons we've learned?

Could it be that we have forgotten exactly where we are?

That we live in the fallen world where sometimes things *look* bizarre.

Can we judge the right or wrong path for the guiding wind to blow

When we are like a sailor headed for a port we don't know?

Before we complain to God about all we appear to lose,

Maybe we should remember that He gave us the freedom to choose.

We can choose to let our problems bring us down or make us strong.

We can trust God and that He has a purpose for all that *seems* wrong.

God is the Creator. He is all-powerful and all good.

Not only is He willing to destroy sin, but also He surely could.

Where should He begin? Where would you have the Lord God start?

Should He begin with you and the unspoken sins of your heart?

You see, Adam is not the only one who's guilty of sin.

Each and every one of us has been tempted and given in.

It's our choice to believe Christ that we have a huge debt to pay

And see the beauty: that He paid it with
what *seemed* to be His worst day.

From God's Own Word

"And the God of all grace, who called you to His eternal glory
in Christ, after you have suffered a little while, will Himself
restore you and make you strong, firm and steadfast. To Him
be the power for ever and ever. Amen" (1 Peter 5:10–11).

"Trust in the Lord with all your heart and lean not
on your own understanding" (Proverbs 3:5).

"He set my feet on a rock and gave me a
firm place to stand" (Psalms 40:2).

"Salvation is found in no one else, for there is no other name under
heaven given to men by which we must be saved" (Acts 4:12).

Dear Little Tristen

DEAR LITTLE TRISTEN, SO SWEET, SO DEAR
WHY DID THE LORD SEND YOU HERE
YOU WERE ONLY HERE A SHORT WHILE
WE BARELY DID SEE YOUR PRECIOUS SMILE

I JUST CANT BELIEVE IT CAN BE TRUE
THAT HE WAS SENT TO ME AND YOU
ONLY TO CAUSE TEARS, TO CAUSE PAIN
BUT TO BRING A MESSAGE FOR OUR GAIN

A WORD FROM THE LORD UP ABOVE
A MESSAGE OF HOPE AND OF LOVE
SO KEEP HOLDING ON, ONE DAY TO SEE
HE PLANTED SOME SEEDS FOR YOU AND ME

HIS WORK ON EARTH TOOK JUST A SHORT WHILE
A BLESSING FOR HIM TO SEE THE LORDS SMILE
WE'LL FILL OUR HEARTS WITH LOVE WHILE WE WAIT
TILL WE MEET AGAIN AT THOSE PEARLY GATES

UNTIL THEN:
HE'LL BE WITH HIS MOMMA WHERE EVER SHE GOES
HE'LL BE WITH HIS DADDY AS HE PLANTS EACH ROSE
HE'LL BE WITH BIG SIS AT ALL OF HER HORSE SHOWS
HE'LL BE WITH BIG BRO WITH EACH BALL HE THROWS

I KNOW THAT
GOD DID SEND THAT ANGEL LITTLE BOY
TO BRING US HAPPINESS, LOVE AND JOY
SO PLEASE KEEP YOUR FAITH IN GOD ABOVE
HE'LL BRING YOU HOPE AND LOTS OF LOVE

From God's Own Word

Trust the Lord with all
your heart and lean not
on your own understanding.
Proverbs 3:5

Section Four

Faith and Hope

Faith

What this thing called faith is to me:
It is believing what we can't see.
I heard a saying that I'd like to borrow
For when life brings pain and sorrow.

It has to do with a rainy April day,
So there is hope for flowers in May.
Although it is raining very hard outside
And the sun just seems to run and hide...

Its light won't shine, not even a ray,
And its warmth seems to be so very far away.
It is still there above the dark skies,
Even if we can't see it with our eyes.

So it is with God's Son,
The Lord Jesus, the Holy One.

When the storms of life come today,
Without a doubt, we can truly say,
Although we can't feel His warmth right now
And His light is dim, we know somehow

He is still there above the dark skies,
Even if we can't see Him with our eyes.
So please keep your faith in God above.
He will bless you with *His* hope and love.

And hang onto faith, even small as a seed.
In heaven, there won't be a single weed.
But all of our flowers, pretty as can be,
Are waiting there for you and me.

From God's Own Word

"Now faith is being sure of what we hope for and certain of what we do not see" (Hebrews 11:1).

"Let us fix our eyes on Jesus, the author and perfecter of our faith" (Hebrews 12:2).

Faith and Trust

I have been thinking of something that I heard long ago
About what it means to have faith and how God makes it grow.
I heard that faith is the ability to see in the dark.
It's finding your way in the dark without even a spark.

Faith is trusting God even when we don't understand why
Our eyes are blinded from the darkness and the tears we cry.
It's believing, when we can't see the reason for our test,
That Jesus will dry our tears and give us His peace and rest.

Faith is believing that God will use each dark and gloomy pit
To bring forth a strength and hope from which we can benefit.
It is trusting in God's wisdom, power, mercy, and grace,
Knowing that He would not allow a useless or needless dark space.

Faith is trusting God, with a heart and mind that is humble,
That He will not let us fall—though at times we may stumble.
It's believing that He is always there to offer His hand
And to make our steps firm, upholding us until we can stand.

Though no one likes hardship, we can rejoice while we're in pain,
Trusting that God will use our circumstance for a worthy gain.
Remember—if not for the darkness, we could not know the light.
We would never put our hand out for the Lord to hold tight.

From God's Own Word

"In this you greatly rejoice, though now for a little while you may have had to suffer grief in all kinds of trials. These have come so your faith—of greater worth than gold, which perishes even though refined by fire—may be proved genuine and may result in praise, glory and honor when Jesus Christ is revealed" (1 Peter 1:6–7).

The Light of Hope

When you're feeling abandoned, frightened, broken, and weak,
And comfort from pain and heartache is all that you seek,
Remember—first, there was darkness before there was light,
And the morning always comes *after* the dark of night.
So, when day breaks and after the morning star appears,
The sun will rise, and its warmth will dry your dewy tears.

Like the pain that comes with childbirth is soon forgotten,
So will our grief when we're dressed in white, soft as cotton.
For what we can't see right now, what is out of our sight,
Will be revealed when the Lord God comes to shine His light.
So we must persevere and wait for the promised day
When the light of hope helps us see life in a new way.

From God's Own Word

"May the God of hope fill you with all joy and peace as you trust in Him, so that you may overflow with hope by the power of the Holy Spirit" (Romans 15:13).

"Find rest, O my soul, in God alone; my hope comes from Him" (Psalms 62:5).

Our Ever-Present Help

I've been thinking of an interpretation that I heard
Of a story that I read in the Bible, the Lord's own Word.
It really made me think of this story in a new way,
About this Man Jesus whom even the stormy winds must obey.

Jesus just fed thousands with two fish and five loaves of bread
When He made His disciples get in the boat and go on ahead.
Then Jesus dismissed the crowd so each could go their own way.
After leaving them, He went up a mountainside to pray.

The boat was in the middle of the lake when evening came.
Jesus was on land but could see the disciples' toil just the same.
He could see them straining at the oars because of the wind,
So, walking on the water, He went out to make the winds rescind.

But when the disciples saw Jesus walking on the lake,
They were so terrified that they began to cry out, tremble, and quake.
They did not realize it was Him; they thought He was a ghost.
"Take courage! It is I. Don't be afraid," Jesus quickly spoke without boast.

Then Jesus climbed in with them to calm the wind and their fears,
For no matter where we are when we're in trouble, He sees and hears.
When He climbs in with us, the winds must obey His command,
So keep your faith in stormy winds that He will help you withstand.

Not only does this story show we are never too far
For God to see our strife, it also shows He climbs in—wherever we are.
And though we may lose sight of Him, He won't lose sight of us.
He'll come and care for us, our ever-present help, the Lord Jesus.

From God's Own Word

"'Take courage! It is I. Don't be afraid.' Then He climbed in the boat with them, and the wind died down" (Mark 6:50–51).

"God is our refuge and strength, an ever-present help in trouble" (Psalms 46:1).

Tapestry

Life as compared to a tapestry,
With only one side that we can see.
We see a lot of knots and loose thread
That seem to leave so much unsaid.

God is looking from the other side.
"It is finished." He smiles with pride.
He doesn't see the knots or loose thread,
But a beautiful picture He sees instead.

When we wonder and when we doubt
What life in this world is all about,
Remember all that the good Lord said:
He won't leave any knots or loose thread.

And when that needle again pokes through,
It is not meant to cause damage to you,
But it is to bring forth a new thread,
To complete the picture He sees instead.

Trust the Lord with all of your might,
And He will shine His heavenly light.
Let Him snip the knots and loose thread.
Allow Him to ease your worry and dread.

It doesn't seem to make sense right now,
But when it's complete, it will somehow.
We won't see the knots or loose thread,
But the beautiful picture God sees instead.

From God's Own Word

"And we know that in all things God works for the good of those who *love Him*, who have been called according to His purpose" (Romans 8:28, emphasis added).

"Trust the Lord with all your heart and lean not on your own understanding" (Proverbs 3:5).

Storms

I have been thinking

about the crux of the horrible and bad,

The events in our lives that make us feel

scared, hopeless, and sad.

There is so much disaster

that we really don't understand,

Like when devastation strikes

here at home or in a foreign land.

Storms can come

in tornado, tsunami, or hurricane form.

Hardship can blow in

as one of many different kinds of storm.

Some of our storms come from the Earth,
when the land slides or quakes,

And others appear when

an entire mountain spews lava and shakes.

Torrents might come through flooding
rain, raging seas, or fire water.,
It might be an act of God or mankind,
an illness or manslaughter.
Disaster can fall on us
in the shape of snow, hail, or sleet
And make the paths we travel
dangerous for our wheels and feet.

Total destruction can happen
when a lone spark ignites a fire.
It can shoot through a gun in war,
randomly, or a killer for hire.
Though we don't always know why, we
must face these terrible storms.
We do know that every storm brings about changes.
It transforms.

As each storm passes,

we can better prepare ourselves for the next.

Our storms help to build faith in God, not
just to leave our minds perplexed.

Whether it's water, earth, wind, mankind,
or fire, the next time you feel frail,

Ask God to help build your faith, hope, and
strength—and you will prevail.

The Lord is our refuge and strength,

as said in the forty-sixth psalm.

He says to know that He's God, He's in control,
and that we should be calm.

He is our ever-present help in trouble—

therefore, do not fear.

The Lord is with us during storms and
will bless those who persevere.

From God's Own Word

"God is our refuge and our strength, an ever-present help in trouble. Therefore we will not fear, though the earth give way and the mountains fall into the heart of the sea, though its waters roar and foam and the mountains quake with their surging" (Psalms 46:1–3).

"Be still and know that I am God" (Psalms 46:8–10).

The Mountains We Climb

I read somewhere recently

about the mountains that we climb.

They might come our way

if we're the victim of a crime,

Or perhaps through an injury or illness

that seems to never end,

Or the death of a precious child,

close family member, or friend.

It said something like

when climbing up a mountain, stay steadfast,

For God sees over the peak—

the prize that will forever last.

We gain not only a reward, but also more

strength from climbing uphill.

Downhill is nice,

but we don't build our faith, endurance, and skill.

Please try to persevere

and wait for the promise of the Lord.

Your time of hardship, tears, and pain
will bring with it God's reward.

There is a time

for mountaintops and for the valleys below,

But no matter where you are,

the Lord is with you where you go.

From God's Own Word

"There is a time for everything, and a season for every activity under heaven... a time to weep and a time to laugh, a time to mourn and a time to dance" (Ecclesiastes 3:1,4).

"For everything that was written in the past was written to teach us, so that through endurance and the encouragement of the Scriptures we might have hope" (Romans 15:4).

Rolling On

Sometimes I feel like I'm a bucket filled with water
Instead of a mom, a wife, or Mom and Dad's daughter.
It's like I'm being poured out—then down the hill I race,
Seeking my own level, anxious to find the base,
Just to be vaporized and then wait for the rain to pour.
So I can get to racing down that hill once more.

Or, I'm, a waterfall that rumbles over the edge.
It travels over and around every nook and wedge.
No rock in the way on this winding obstacle course
Could stop the water from flowing with a mighty force.
Then, just before it takes the plunge, it rolls to the end,
Embracing the fate to which it's about to descend.

At times, I think I'm more like a babbling brook
That chatters on and on about my life's outlook,
Winding through the trees in harmony with the songbirds,
All singing praises to the Lord with songs that have no words.
Crashing against each rock I meet, before moving on,
I roll toward each new day, forgetting those long gone.

Then there are the days when I feel like I'm a tranquil stream,
Though it's not very often I live this peaceful dream.
Water drifts along so smooth. I can't see it move,
Gliding over each stone with *not a thing* to prove.
It blesses each stone and pebble with a gracious smile,
Then rolls on seeking peace and silence—mile after mile.

Some days, I feel like I'm an ocean or a vast sea.
I believe I'm all-powerful; there's no stopping me!
Then there are the days I feel like a muddy puddle.
Everything I do, say, and touch, I botch and muddle.
Sometimes I feel like ducts, so full of tears I could burst,
And others, like an ice-cold drink that could quench any thirst.

Whatever life brings, no matter how the water rolls,
I'm glad to know that someone else operates the controls.
Whether I'm like a raging sea or a country pond,
There's One who carries me through the waters and beyond.
That someone is God. He is the river that sustains.
He's the River that washes away my sinful stains.

From God's Own Word

"When you pass through the waters, I will be with you; and when you pass through the rivers, they will not sweep over you" (Isaiah 43:2).

A New Heart

When your heart is sick, or it aches because it's broke,
Remember those words that were long ago spoke.
God said that when we talk to Him, He always hears.
He says that He hears our prayers and sees our tears.

Even though He has seen our ways, He will heal us.
God will restore and comfort if we turn to Jesus.
He is compassionate and will hear our cries.
He will respond and dry the tears from our eyes.

There are many reasons a heart might need repair,
Such as a heart attack, loneliness, or despair.
It could be the pain of losing someone you love
Or a combination of all the above.

Your heart might hurt because of where you are,
If you've turned away from God and wandered afar.
Maybe you forgot or don't know how good it feels
To be filled with the Spirit of the One who heals.

If your heart aches and you're looking for a friend,
Someone to comfort and heal, someone who can mend,
Then turn to Jesus. He will give you a new heart,
Putting a new spirit inside you for a new start.

From God's Own Word

"I will give you a new heart and put a new spirit in you" (Ezekiel 36:26).

This River

There is a river that flows, made of grief and sorrow's tears.
It has been rolling since the dawn of history's years.
Who can stop the roaring and rising of this deathly beast?
There seems to be no one able, not for now, at least.

Even though the Lord has overcome the Devil's plan,
We must wait for His return for the redemption of man.
Then He will stop the surging of all these tears we cry.
He will wipe every tear, and then this river will run dry.

There will come a time of comfort, the break of a new day,
When the order of death and mourning will pass away.
Though for now it seems that we'll drown in this tear-filled flood,
We have a promise that's sealed with the Lord's precious blood.

For there is another river, one with grace-filled swells.
It is in a city where the Most High's presence dwells.
Therefore, do not fear, though the earth's waters roar and foam,
Because Jesus promised He would return to take us home.

And when that day comes, we'll see this river face-to-face.
The source of our hope and strength is a river called Grace.
Now, we see murky water with its reflection so poor,
But through this River of Life, we clearly see heaven's door.

From God's Own Word

"He will wipe every tear from their eyes. There will be no more death or mourning or crying or pain, for the old order of things has passed away" (Revelation 21:4).

Lemons

When the world hands us lemons, life turns sour—it's not all that great.
They might come as one lemon or as a whole bunch in a crate.
At times, it seems that a huge truckload gets dumped out on us,
But it's up to us to choose what we'll do with the citrus.

Some people begin right away, digging their own selves out.
And others wait for someone else; they just sit there and pout.
Some try to find something good they can do with the sour fruit.
Perhaps they can add some sweetness, grate the peels, or dilute.

Yes, sometimes life hands out lemons. But it also provides
Many different ways to use them—to help us make great strides.
We can use the juice to oust smells like stinky sardine
Or add it to cleaners to make everything sparkling clean.

You can squeeze the juice into the recipes you like best.
It gives any dish, sauce, dessert, or drink a special zest.
The lemons' color alone is enough to brighten any room;
It's like the sun is shining in just to brighten life's gloom.

When life hands out lemons, you can make a refreshing treat.
You could add any kind of berry for a bit of sweet.
Or mix them with water, sugar, and milk for lemonade,
Then open up a stand and sell the sweet nectar you made.

The next time you're handed lemons, will you up and pucker
Or turn it into something sweet, like a lemon sucker?
Will you begin digging, or will you just sit there and mope?
Will you turn the sour into good with the sweet taste of hope?

From God's Own Word

"May the God of hope fill you with all joy and peace as you trust in Him, so that you may overflow with hope by the power of the Holy Spirit" (Romans 15:13).

The Risen Son

I walked with the rising sun, up and down the beach,
Searching for certain seashells for which I might reach.
I thought of times past and of how I used to be,
Only taking the "perfect" shells released from the sea.

But my sight has changed, and so has my interest.
Now I search for shells that are different from the rest.
I see it's those shells that have weathered many a storm.
They show strength and endurance in their unique form.

They have withstood strong currents and the crashing surf
Before they were washed on the ocean's sandy turf,
Where they wait to be chosen, to picked up from the shore,
Or to fade away—to remain nevermore.

As I searched through the shells washed in from the sea,
I realized how similar they are to you and me.
As life's stormy wind and waves change our sight and form,
They etch in our souls faith and hope to withstand each storm.

With each step I took on the boundary for the tide,
I could feel the Lord's presence right there by my side.
Overwhelmed, my tears began to swell just to know
That the risen Son walks with me... even when storms blow.

From God's Own Word

"Where can I go from Your Spirit? Where can I
flee from Your presence" (Psalms 139:7)?

"I made the sand a boundary for the sea, an everlasting
barrier it cannot cross" (Jeremiah 5:22).

Walking on Water

The Lord Jesus will surely keep us afloat
If we will trust Him and get out of the boat.
We can walk on water if we focus on Him,
When the wind and waves seem hopeless and grim.

If we focus more on the storm that surrounds us
Than on the mighty power of the Lord Jesus,
Then, without a doubt, we will despair and sink low
And also miss the beauty of His awesome rainbow.

After the storm, there'll be a rainbow in the skies.
It can only be seen when we focus our eyes
On the One who can help, with His divine power,
To restore our faith in our most doubtful hour.

And though we may never know the reasons for sure
For the hardships we sometimes have to endure,
We have His promise of hope to hang onto,
For He says, "I will strengthen you and help you."

So, don't give up on faith and trust just yet.
We can walk on water without getting wet.
The Lord has the power to keep us afloat,
If we trust Him enough to get out of the boat.

From God's Own Word

"Then Peter got down out of the boat, walked on the water and came toward Jesus. But when he saw the wind, he was afraid and, beginning to sink, cried out, 'Lord, save me!' Immediately Jesus reached out His hand and caught him. 'You of little faith,' He said, 'why did you doubt'" (Matthew 14:29–31)?

Lord, What Would You Say?

Lord, what would you say to those who
suffer with heartache and pain,

Whose lives were turned upside down, and,
it seems no faith or hope remains?

What words could you possible say that
would comfort and/or explain

That, concealed in their troubles, there's an eternal glory to gain?

What could be said to comfort those whose loved one has been slain,

Shot to death in a war or by someone driving down the lane?

Or to the parents of a child whose death seems unfair and insane?

What words could make sense of the
senseless in their heart and brain?

Lord, what would you say to the friends and families that remain

After terrorists strike for reasons that are completely profane?

When thousands die in towers hit with bombs the size of airplanes,

Are there any words strong enough to
remove this kind of bloodstain?

What about those who feel they're drowning in a never-ending rain

Or that they're going down for the third
time, with no strength to regain?

Lord, what would you say to those who
suffer with heartache and pain,

Whose lives were turned upside down and
it seems no faith or hope remain?

What about those lives taken by drugs such as heroine or cocaine,

Or, any other substance they drink, smoke,
snort or shoot in their vein?

How can we understand the power of this unbreakable chain?

What words can help us grasp why they were never able to sustain?

Lord, what would you say to those whose five
loved ones seemed to die in vain?

Dear God, Father of compassion, comfort
their grieving tears and pain.

Please remind them of the hope they have in Your eternal domain

Where there's no more tears, forever, and
where You and Your glory reign.

From God's Own Word

"The Lord is close to the brokenhearted" (Psalms 35:18).

"Praise be to the God and Father of our Lord Jesus Christ, the Father of compassion and the God of all comfort, who comforts us in all our troubles" (2 Corinthians 1:3–4).

"Jesus wept" (John 11:35).

Who Told You?

Who was it that told you this outlandish lie?
Was it he who said, "You will not surely die"?
Was it the same one? Does he have the same name
As the one who caused Adam and Eve their shame?

Who said that all in life would come sweet and easy,
That your skies would always be sunny and breezy,
Your parade never dampened with rain,
And your heart never cry tears or feel pain?

Who told your life's worth and all of your joys
Would come by having the most and the best toys?
That life is about being happy and free?
Who was it that gave you the false guarantee

That you would never have to sweat or work hard
To take care of your family, home, or yard,
That you'd never come face-to-face with bad intent,
That neither you nor your wallet could be completely spent?

Who do you know that never deals with sad?
Who is living the life you wish you had had?
You better take a closer look and think twice.
I promise you'll find things that are not so nice.

Even if life was like a bowl of cherries,
We'd still have the pits that come inside berries.
There would still be the stem from which the fruit grew
To remind us that sweet can become a sour brew.

You can take the fruit life grows for you each day
And use it in your own very special way.
You can make a sweet nectar to share with all
Or an evil juice that answers Satan's call.

God never promised us a life with no grief
Or a long life. In fact, sometimes lives are very brief.
He never said He'd put us in a bubble
That would protect us from pain, harm, or trouble.

He did promise though that He'd be with us always,
Even on those "Life is the pits" kind of days.
He said He would help us, so don't be afraid.
Please, trust the Lord and the promises He made.

From God's Own Word

"I have told you these things, so that in Me you may
have peace. In this world you will have trouble. But take
heart! I have overcome the world" (John 16:33)!

God Is Good

In nineteen seventy-nine, my entire life changed.
In a split second, my whole life was rearranged.
I was twenty-two; my brother Carl was seventeen.
He was driving on a curve where his car would careen.

We were sleeping when the call came from my dad.
He said that Carl was in a wreck that was really bad.
He said, "Carl died in the crash—his neck had been broken."
We could not believe the words that my dad had spoken.

The shock confused me. I didn't know where to start.
How could I even breathe with this pain in my heart?
The ache was so bad I thought my heart would just stop,
And my knees were so weak I thought they'd let me drop.

The word *heartache* was not just a word anymore;
It was now a reality that stood at my door.
"God is good" is what people would always tell me,
But I wondered, *If God is so good, how can this be?*

If God is so good, why would He cause all these tears?
How could He allow this fulfillment of my worst fears?
I was so mad at God that I stopped believing in Him.
I moved away from God—and grew closer to sin.

Then, one day, there was something that turned me around.
The Lord asked me a question I thought to be profound:
"How can you be mad at someone you don't believe in?"
In that second, I realized how foolish I had been.

The hardest part of life is when we have to face death,
Whether it's our own or someone else's last breath.
But one thing I have learned from tragedies so grim:
There is always hope if we draw nearer to Him.

Things happen in our lives that we would never choose,
But we are the ones who decide if we win or lose.
We can let God make good things come from these tragedies
If we choose to overcome with the right strategies.

Come near to God, and He will come near to you.
He will comfort your pain and renew your strength, too.
Ask Him to come live in your heart, to please never leave.
He will restore the faith and hope of those who believe.

Some memories are so close, they seem like yesterday;
Others have faded to a place that is far away.
It takes time to heal, but if we ask God to live within,
He will work all things for the good of those who love Him.

From God's Own Word

"And we know that in all things God works for the good of those who love Him" (Romans 8:28).

"But those who hope in the Lord will renew their strength" (Isaiah 40:31).

Trust in Him

Where are You, Lord, when I need You the most?
It seems as if I've searched from coast to coast.
I've looked up high for the path that You go
And searched for You in the valley below.

Why would You leave me now, just disappear,
After You promised that You would draw near?
You said that You would never leave me all alone.
Where are You, dear Lord? Where have You gone?

You told me this world would be troublesome
But to take heart because You have overcome!
You promised to carry me through, all the way;
You would be with me each and every day.

Where are You, Lord, when I need You the most?
You said that to peace and comfort, You're the host.
You asked me to trust and have faith in You
Because Your promise is certain, it is true.

I did forget to look in one other place.
It's where You fill me with Your love and grace.
Your promise is true; You never depart.
You were here all along, here in my heart.

From God's Own Word

"You will seek me and find me when you seek me
with all your heart" (Jeremiah 29:13).

"Do not let your hearts be troubled. Trust in
God; trust also in me" (John 14:1).

Trust

Suppose you're in your boat just cruising along—and all is fine.
Then, all of a sudden, a strong wind starts to howl and whine.
Your vessel begins to shift and toss, and the waves churn about.
There are storm clouds rolling in that stir up worry and doubt.

As the sky grows darker, you can see every lightning streak.
With each roar of thunder, the situation becomes more bleak.
You begin to seek shelter before the rain begins to pour,
Anxious to find a safe spot—but there's no harbor on the shore.

So you set the anchor and batten down all the hatches,
Making sure everything is secured with the ropes and latches.
You put your trust in the Lord and pray that His will be done.
Then you go down below to wait for the return of the sun.

Well, that's the way life is sometimes as we're cruising along.
Everything seems great, but then, all at once, it starts to go wrong.
Everything seems to snowball, with no real reason to explain,
And suddenly you feel stranded, alone with the wind and rain.

But we're never alone; God promised to always be with us.
So, batten down the hatches and ride out this storm with Jesus.
He gives us strength to endure life's squalls. He gives all that we need,
Even when our faith and trust are as small as a mustard seed.

He is *the anchor* during life's storms that holds us in place.
He is *the ropes and latches* that secure His saving grace.
He is our faith and hope when our lives churn, shift, and toss.
So remember, trust always begins and ends with the cross.

From God's Own Word

"I will put my trust in Him" (Hebrews 2:13).

"Be strong and courageous. Do not be terrified;
do not be discouraged, for the Lord God will be
with you wherever you go" (Joshua 1:9).

"When I am afraid, I will trust in you. In God, whose word I
praise, in God I trust; I will not be afraid" (Psalms 56:3–4).

The Heavy Load

I just read a true story I received from my dear friend Gale.

She had sent it to me through the Internet, in an e-mail.

I just might have doubted this great story if I did not know firsthand

That the eyes of the Lord can truly see everything in this land.

This is how the story goes, although just the thought scares me stiff:

Brenda was almost halfway up a tremendous granite cliff.

She stopped for a breather on a ledge. Then, as she was resting,

The safety rope hit her eye—which proved to be very testing.

This was during her first rock climb. She was aiming for the sky.

The rope knocked out her contact lens

when it snapped against her eye.

Great, she thought, *I'm on a rock ledge, hundreds of feet from the top,*

And I'm hundreds of feet from the bottom, so I can't just stop!

With blurry sight, she looked and looked
for the lens along the ground,

But she began to panic when it was nowhere to be found.

So she prayed that she may find her lens. She also prayed for calm

And thought of this Bible verse, which
would be the base for her psalm:

"The eyes of the Lord run to and fro throughout the whole Earth."

Though it seemed hopeless, she prayed with
her faith for all it was worth:

"Lord, you know every stone and leaf, and
all these mountains You see,

And You know exactly where my contact lens is. Please help me."

Later, her group all hiked down the trail to the bottom of the cliff.,

They met another group of climbers just starting up the cliff.

One of them shouted out, "Anybody lose a contact lens?"

Wow, I can only imagine the praise, thank-yous, and amens!

If that weren't startling enough, guess where it was? I bet you can't.

Slowly moving across a twig, there was just a common ant

There on the face of the rock, carrying the lens on its back!

But that's not the end of this ant's unusual luggage rack.

When she told her cartoonist dad of the awesome episode,

He drew a cartoon of an ant carrying a see-through load.

With the words, "Lord, why You want me
to lug this weight, I don't know,

But I will for You. And I know You'll give me the strength to do so."

What we learn from this heavily burdened ant that slowly crawled

Is this: God doesn't call the qualified, He qualifies the called.

Yes, I love God. Without Him, I'm nothing, which I plainly see,

But with Him, I can do all things, for it's Christ who strengthens me.

I think it would do us all some good if we looked to the sky

And said, "God, I see no good in this load, or the reason why.

I can't see who or what will benefit from this load, but still,

Just because it is You who asks me to carry it, I will."

And this story is a portrayal for all of us to see

That God is with us in the deepest of the valleys and the sea.

He is there in the water we cross and the mountains we climb.

He proves His love and provides for all our needs, time after time.

From God's Own Word

"I can do all things through Christ who strengthens me" (Philippians 4:13).

"And my God will meet all your needs according to His glorious riches in Christ Jesus" (Philippians 4:19).

Give Me Strength

During those times when it seems like you're all alone,
When it feels like you're completely unknown,
You think there's no one that can see or hear you
And that nothing is right—nothing you say or do.

It seems like you're in a dark tunnel
Or your head is spinning, as if in a funnel,
And there's no one to make the darkness end
Or stop the spinning. There's not even one friend.

When you don't think the rain will ever stop
And it feels like you're drowning with every drop,
Remember that, like a flower, we can't see how the rain
Will make us grow, or how much strength we will gain.

So, when you're lost and confused and filled with fright,
Don't give up. Keep searching till you see the light.
When your life feels like it's spinning out of control,
There is a power that will steady your heart and soul.

So, never give in—never give up on faith or hope!
There is one who'll give you all that's needed to cope.
Just call out His name and say to Him, "Give me strength."
He will give more than enough to go any length.

The Lord Jesus will give us strength if we ask.
He will provide all that's needed for every task.
He will never allow more than we can bear
Or leave us alone when life seems most unfair.

From God's Own Word

Do you not know? Have you not heard? The Lord is the everlasting God, the Creator of the ends of the earth. He will not grow tired or weary, and His understanding no one can fathom. He gives strength to the weary and increases the power of the weak. Even youths grow tired and weary, and young men stumble and fall; but those who hope in the Lord will renew their strength. They will soar on wings like eagles; they will run and not grow weary, they will walk and not be faint. (Isaiah 40:28–31)

Forever So Bright

When it seems you're in the darkest hour of night
And there seems to be no light shining bright,
When you look to the sky for a glimpse of starlight,
But all you can see is a dark, gloomy plight...

When the wall you scale is the highest of height
And the current you swim flows with rapid might,
When the tears you have cried have blurred your sight
Or your wings have broken during your flight...

When you have no strength but still have to fight
And the weakness has diminished your insight,
When all your colors turn to black, even the white,
Or the wind you're flying in turns your plane upright...

When you're lonely, with no loved one to reunite,
And when sadness and depression allow no delight,
When the storm looming over is causing great fright
Or the clouds roll in and rob your life of daylight...

When you have been lured by a sinful appetite
And your actions have made your heart contrite,
When heartache is your only bedfellow at night
Or it seems your world was blown up with dynamite...

Remember:
In the darkest hour of the long, cold night,
The sun is still shining forever so bright,
And it will rise again with His glorious light
To shine upon you and brighten your gloomy plight.

From God's Own Word

"You, O Lord, keep my lamp burning; my God turns my darkness into light. With Your help I can advance against a troop; with my God I can scale a wall" (Psalms 18:28–29).

The Bright Side

The bright side is always the side that the Lord is on.
Darkness is the side where all our faith and hope have gone.
In Him, there is no darkness at all, for God *is* light,
So look to Him when you need to see a side that's bright.

He's like the light that brings the grass after rain showers
And the brightness that brings forth the pretty spring flowers.
He's like the light that breaks through to reveal a rainbow
And burns away storm clouds, exposing a warm glow.

He is the light shining in our hearts so we can teach
That, through Christ Jesus, salvation is within our reach.
He's like the light at sunrise on a cloudless morning
And the star that rises in the midst of our mourning.

His light can dry the rain that is falling from the sky.
It can also dry the painful tears that we cry.
It can melt away all the ice that threatens our pace
And then heat the coldness with a warm, loving embrace.

He is the light that puts faith and hope within our sight.
No matter how dark the tunnel, we will see His light.
So, when our picture of life seems dark, hopeless, and dim,
The *Son* will reveal the bright side if we turn to Him.

From God's Own Word

"He is like the light of the morning at sunrise on a cloudless morning, like the brightness after rain that brings the grass from the Earth" (2 Samuel 23:4).

Hang Tough

What has been on my mind lately, more than it ever has before,

Makes me feel so bewildered that it drops my knees to the floor.

It is the pain and suffering that we sometimes have to endure,

The kind that grinds at our souls, leaving us weak and insecure.

The pain might be physical or emotional, or maybe it's both.

It hits hard—and all at once—during seasons of spiritual growth.

At times, it seems as though we must have fallen under a curse.

Things get so bad, we can't imagine that they could get much worse.

We wonder, *What good could possibly come from this, and how?*
And it's hard to hang on to *future* hope when we're in pain right now.

We can't see how God will use each struggle to refine us like gold,

The way fire heats gold to purify it and make it easier to mold.

When we are in the valley with what seems to be no way out

And our faith and hope are replaced with fear, despair, and doubt,

We must remember that God can see over the mountains we climb.

He sees the reward that awaits us, that's
why He allows these trying times.

There are numerous reasons why we have hardship and pain,

And countless lessons to be learned—all from which we can gain.

And, though we may not know the reasons while living this life,

With God's power, we have a living hope
through faith in the new birth.

There's hope in knowing that God will use
it for good, whatever the strife.

When we feel the most like giving up, *that*
is when we should hang tough,

For, in His perfect time, God will make
smooth the peaks that are rough.

He will Himself restore you and make you
strong, firm, and steadfast.

I encourage you with the true grace of God that you stand fast.

From God's Own Word

"And the God of all grace, who called you to His eternal glory in Christ, after you have suffered a little while, will Himself restore you and make you strong, firm and steadfast. To Him be the power for ever and ever. Amen" (1 Peter 5:10–11).

"I have written to you briefly, encouraging you and testifying that this is the true grace of God. Stand fast in it" (1 Peter 5:12).

Section Five

Prayers

Answered Prayers

How do we know for sure the Lord hears our prayers?
How can we tell if He even really cares?
Can we know if He takes notice when we pray
And if His answer will make it all okay?

Does it depend on the mood He might be in,
Or if He feels we're "good enough," free of sin?
Is there some sort of method or secret code
That gives prayers higher rank, like a pious ode?

Should we stand, sit, or kneel so He can better hear us?
Should we call Him Father, God, Lord, or Jesus?
Is it better to pray inside a pretty church
So He won't snub us and leave us on the lurch?

How can we be sure that our prayers He will heed
And know that He'll answer with the fastest of speed?
Can we do or say something special for Him
To be certain that we're assured of our every whim?

There is nothing special we need do or say,
And we don't need to be in a church to pray.
It doesn't matter if we stand, sit, or kneel.
We can call the direct line any time we feel.

And not only does God hear each and every prayer,
But He also answers each one. Just beware:
We don't always get the answer for which we pine,
Nor does His timing always fit in our time line.

But of this one fact we can certainly be sure:
In the midst of crisis, He will help us endure.
We must trust that His answer is the one we need
And that the timing is perfect, coming with God's speed.

From God's Own Word

"Call to Me and I will answer you" (Jeremiah 33:3).

"Wait patiently for the Lord. Be brave and courageous. Yes, wait patiently for the Lord" (Psalms 27:14).

Give Thanks

We ask God to give us this and help us with that,
And call Him when we're lonely, just needing to chat.
We ask for His protection while we're on our way
Or for help when we have overdue bills to pay.

We ask for sunshine when our skies are overcast.
Then we need rain when it's dry—and we need it fast.
We ask for quick answers to all our urgent prayers,
And we ask Him to remove all our heavy cares.

We ask Him to help buy a new car or dream house,
And we ask Him to send us a *trouble-free* spouse.
We ask for perfect children, a girl and a boy.
Or how about a job that brings rest, peace, and joy?

We ask for "yes" answers to all the pleas we've cried,
Wanting only to be content and satisfied.
We ask and we ask, sometimes forgetting to say
Please and *thank you* for the blessings sent our way.

Now and then, He'll ask for a moment of our time,
Or to share with others, maybe even a dime.
But we're much too busy with building a career,
So how could we give the money we hold so dear?

We can't seem to find a spare minute of our day
Or something small left from our hard-earned pay
To show the Lord we're grateful for all that He's done,
Like paying our sin's debt with the blood of His Son.

From God's Own Word

"You are my God, and I will give you thanks; you are my God, and I will exalt you. Give thanks to the Lord, for He is good; His love endures forever" (Psalms 118:29).

Dear Holy Father

Lord, I praise and worship Your holy name,
Though I am unworthy and laden with shame.
I come before You today full of sin—
So full that I don't even know where to begin.

May I please approach Your heavenly throne
To confess to You that I am evil-prone?
I ask You, Father, to please forgive me,
Even though I am not worthy of this plea.

I pray that You help me forgive others,
As you've forgiven me and my brothers.
I offer myself to You this day
As a servant unworthy in every way.

I ask that Your most perfect will be done,
And also that Your spiritual kingdom will come,
That You give me today my daily bread
And lead me from Satan's lures of sin and dread.

Jesus, I thank you for your suffering,
For the grace and mercy your flesh and blood bring,
For taking my sins and nailing them tight,
Covering them with your blood, out of God's sight.

From God's Own Word

"If we confess our sins, He is faithful and just and will forgive us our sins and purify us from all unrighteousness" (1 John 1:9).

On Your Knees

Pray from where you are when life brings you down to your knees.
It's a good place to start, and you have to start somewhere.
God's compassion will come to you like a gentle breeze.

When you're encumbered with troubles like death and disease,
Call to God. He will comfort you when He hears your prayer.
Pray from where you are when life brings you down to your knees.

If you're overwhelmed with turmoil and there's no appease,
If you feel trapped and need to be released from this snare,
God's compassion will come to you like a gentle breeze.

When you're drowning in debt and all your bills have late fees,
When there's nothing in your bank account, nothing to spare,
Pray from where you are when life brings you down to your knees.

Whether you're burdened with all kinds of grief such as these
Or you struggle with loneliness, sadness, and despair,
God's compassion will come to you like a gentle breeze.

When you're weighed down with misery and can find no ease,
You need someone to help you carry the cross you bear.
Pray from where you are when life brings you down to your knees.

From God's Own Word

"Answer me when I call to You, O my righteous
God. Give me relief from my distress; be merciful
to me and hear my prayer" (Psalms 4:1).

And I Pray

I will kneel before the Father and pray
That He will strengthen your faith to get through this day,
Providing the power to endure whatever comes your way.
For this reason, I kneel before Him, and I pray.

I will kneel before the Father and pray
That He will strengthen you in your innermost being
So Christ may dwell in your heart, through faith never fleeing.
For this reason, I kneel before Him, and I pray.

I will kneel before the Father and pray
That He will give you the power to grasp Christ's love.
How wide and long, how high and deep, is this love from above.
For this reason, I kneel before Him, and I pray.

I will kneel before the Father and pray
That you might know this love that surpasses all knowledge,
That you may be filled to the fullest with this privilege.
For this reason, I kneel before Him, and I pray.

I will kneel before the Father and pray
That He will guide you as you journey through this day.
I ask Him to walk before you to show you the way.
For this reason, I kneel before Him, and I pray.

I will kneel before the Father and pray
That He will bless you with His presence in your heart,
So you know *nothing* could ever tear you two apart.
For this reason, I kneel before Him, and I pray.

From God's Own Word

For this reason I kneel before the Father, from whom His whole family in heaven and on earth derives its name. I pray that out of His glorious riches He may strengthen you with power through His Spirit in your inner being, so that Christ may dwell in your hearts through faith. And I pray that you, being rooted and established in love, may have power, together with all the saints, to grasp how wide and long and high and deep is the love of Christ, and to know this love that surpasses knowledge—that you may be filled to the measure of all the fullness of God. (Ephesians 3:14–19)

Please Use These Tears

Please, Lord, use these tears to wash the mud from my eyes
So I can clearly see all the blessings in disguise.
Use them to drown all of the outside worldly noise
So I can hear Your voice and obey with great poise.

If You will, use them to flush the grime from my blood
So Your blood can flow through my veins like a mighty flood.
Lord, use these tears to cleanse my heart of hate and scorn,
So You can fill it with a love that is heaven-born.

Lord, please use these tears to rinse the dust off my feet
So I might bring Your good news to all those that I meet.
Use them to soak the weakness from my feeble hands
So I can carry your grace to peoples in all lands.

Please, Lord, use these tears to moisten my dry, cracked lips
So I cannot speak any mean and sarcastic quips.
Use them to shower the bitterness from my tongue
So Your hymns of praise are the only songs to be sung.

If you'd please, use them to scrub this pain from my heart
So Your peace and love can provide me with a fresh start.
Please use these tears to bathe the anger from mind
So You can use my soul for the good of all humankind.

It's in the precious name of Jesus that I ask. Amen.

From God's Own Word

"Those who sow in tears will reap with songs of joy. He who goes out weeping, carrying seed to sow, will return with songs of joy, carrying sheaves with him" (Psalms 126:5–6).

The Rooster's Crow

Thank you, Father, for this new day
And for all things that will come my way.
Whether it's good or bad, right or wrong,
Please, dear Lord, be with me all day long.

As the rooster crows, announcing the day,
Please light my path; show me the way.
Let Your light shine with its heavenly glow
As this new day dawns with a rooster's crow.

As the sun rises from beneath the eastern sky,
I can see Your glory shine with my own eye.
For all that You have done and are going to do,
I praise Your holy name, Lord, and I love You.

Bless me with forgiveness, Your perfect love,
And fill me with Your Spirit from up above.
Please help my faith in You continue to grow
As this new day dawns with a rooster's crow.

I offer myself to You on this new day.
Show me where to go; tell me what to say
Myself, for the mercy that you have shown.
Thy will be done, Lord, not my own.

When this day ends, and long after the sunset,
Stay through the night; don't leave me yet.
Watch over me and protect me. Let me know
You're still there with another rooster's crow.

I pray in the name of Jesus.
Amen.

From God's Own Word

"When I awake, I am still with you" (Psalms 139:18).

"Never will I leave you; never will I forsake you" (Hebrews 13:5).

Dear Holy Spirit

Dear Holy Spirit, please come dwell in me
So I can see the way the Lord can see.

Dear Holy Spirit, please come and be near
So I can hear the way the Lord can hear.

Dear Holy Spirit, please come fill me from above
So I can love the way the Lord can love.

Dear Holy Spirit, please consume me like fire
So I can desire what the Lord would desire.

Dear Holy Spirit,
Please let my love, praise, and worship begin at
The very center of my being, flow through every
Cell in my body, consuming me completely,
Until it leaves my heart, soul, and mind through
The tips of my fingers and forms a visible expression
Of my love and passion for You on a piece of paper.

Thank you, my holy and precious Lord Jesus,
God in the flesh.

From God's Own Word

"Teach me to do Your will, for You are my God; may Your good Spirit lead me on level ground" (Psalms 143:10).

To Write

What is it, Lord, that You want me to write
In the stillness of this peaceful night?
What is it, Lord, that You want me to say?
Put Your words in my hands. This I pray.

Shall I tell them about all the love
That I have for You, the Lord up above,
Or about the love that You have for me
And how I pray that one day they'll see
Why my heart is so full of this love
For my dear sweet Lord in heaven above?

Shall I tell them about Your heavenly light
That guides my path, both day and night,
Or about all the times that we've shared,
Good and bad, and how You have always cared?
What is it, Lord, that You want me to write
As I speak with my hands on this moonlit night?

Shall I tell them about that day on the tree
When You gave Your life for them and for me?
Or of Your mercy, Your love, and Your grace—
The gift of belonging to your dwelling place?
And how I pray for that day when we will see
The place that You promise to them and to me?

Or should I just
Say "thank You" for all that You've done
To bring all Your children to a family of one?
What is it, Lord, that You want me to write
For You, my sweet Lord, on this blessed night?

From God's Own Word

"Thanks be to God for His indescribable gift" (2 Corinthians 9:15).

"Go into all the world and preach the good
news to all creation" (Mark 16:15).

Whale Tale

I've been thinking about how we can pray no matter where we are,

Even if we have been running from God and have wandered afar.

Please allow me to explain what I mean by telling you a tale

About a man who ran from God and ended up inside a whale.

This man's name was Jonah. God asked him to go to a certain town

To warn the people that He was going to
turn their world upside down.

They would be punished for their wicked
ways unless they would relent.

He should declare that they could receive
forgiveness if they would repent.

But Jonah ran away from the Lord and headed for Tarshish.

His feelings for Nineveh were very hateful and bitterish.

He did not want the people to receive forgiveness from the Lord,

So he found a ship bound for Tarshish, paid
the fare, and climbed aboard.

But the Lord sent a storm; the whole ship
was threatened by a violent wind.

The sailors were afraid and asked *who* had
caused them to be disciplined.

Jonah had told them he was running from
the Lord and trying to hide.

He said the sea would calm down if they'd throw him over the side.

First, the men tried to row back to land; then,
they cried to God with contrite pleas.

Then they took Jonah and threw him over,
and God calmed the raging seas.

But God provided a great fish to swallow Jonah in his fright,

And he was in the belly of the fish for three days and three nights.

From inside the fish, Jonah prayed to the
Lord his God—to thank Him.

He was grateful; he would have drowned if
God had left him alone to swim.

His prayer ended with this, "Salvation comes from the Lord's hand."

And then the Lord told the great fish to vomit Jonah onto dry land.

Then, Jonah obeyed God and went to Nineveh.

He preached for three days.

He proclaimed that Nineveh would be overturned for its evil ways!

The Ninevites believed God—all of them,

from the greatest to the least.

And God had compassion on them because

their evil ways had ceased.

You and I are much like Jonah. We disobey, then try to flee.

But there's nowhere we can go that God can't hear or see.

And we can't stray too far away for the mercy of Christ Jesus.

If we will just repent and turn back to Him, He will forgive us.

From God's Own Word

"Repent, then, and turn to God, so that your
sins may be wiped out" (Acts 3:19).

"When God saw what they did and how they turned from
their evil ways, He had compassion and did not bring upon
them the destruction He had threatened" (Jonah 3:10).

I Am Thankful

O Lord Jesus,
I am thankful for the crown of thorns that You wore
And for the weight of my sins those thorns surely bore.
I'm thankful for Your flesh that they brutally tore
When the soldier's whips cut down to Your very core.

I'm thankful for the nails that pierced Your hands and feet,
And the sword in Your side that proved it was complete.
I'm thankful that no matter how much You were beat,
The Father, Son, and Spirit, sin could not defeat.

I'm thankful that my being sinful and depraved
Could not stand in the way of my soul's being saved.
I'm thankful that the road to heaven has been paved,
And that to You, my King, I'm forever enslaved.

I'm thankful that I can come before my Master,
Like the woman with the jar of alabaster.
I'm thankful that even I, a poetaster,
Could be used as such to bring praise to my Master.

I'm thankful for Jesus whom upon that cross died,
And for my salvation that His sacrifice did provide.
I am thankful that You are always by my side.
May You always be exalted and magnified.

From God's Own Word

"Come, let us sing for joy to the Lord; let us shout aloud to the Rock of our salvation. Let us come before Him with thanksgiving and extol Him with music and song. For the Lord is the great God, the great King above all gods" (Psalms 95:1–3).

Please Use These Tears

Please Lord, use these tears to wash the mud from my eyes,
So I can clearly see all the blessings in disguise.
Use them to drown all of the outside-worldly noise,
So I can hear Your voice, and obey with great poise.

If You will, use them to flush the grime from my blood,
So Your Blood can flow through my veins like a mighty flood.
Lord, use these tears to cleanse my heart of hate and scorn,
So You can fill it with a love that is Heaven-born.

Lord, please use these tears to rinse the dust off my feet,
So I might bring Your Good News to all those that I meet.
Use them to soak the weakness from my feeble hands,
So I can carry Your Grace to peoples in all lands.

Please Lord, use these tears to moisten my dry, cracked lips,
So I cannot speak any mean and sarcastic quips.
Use them to shower the bitterness from my tongue,
So Your hymns of Praise are the only songs to be sung.

If You'd please, use them to scrub this pain from my heart,
So Your peace and love can replace it with a fresh start.
Please use these tears to bathe the anger from mind,
So You can use my Soul for the good of all mankind.
It's in the precious name of Jesus that I ask. Amen

From God's Own Word

Those who sow in tears will reap with songs
of joy. He who goes out weeping,
carrying seed to sow, will return with songs
of joy, carrying sheaves with him.
Psalm 126:5-6

And we know that in all things God works
for the good of those who love Him.
Romans 8:28

All praise to God, the Father of our Lord Jesus Christ.
God is our merciful Father and source of all comfort.
He comforts us in all our troubles so we can comfort others.
2 Corinthians 1:3-4

Section Six

The Great I Am

The Door

Noah was one of the great patriarchs.
God called down and asked him to build an ark.
God was going to send down a vast flood
To wash away the deeds covered in blood.

The world He had created once was Paradise.
Now, it was full of every kind of wicked vice.
The Lord was grieved, and His heart was broken.
No one listened to the words He had spoken.

God gave Noah a pattern for this ark,
Its door left open for all the embark
For all who believed that they could be saved,
Through this open door, from the watery grave.

But they mocked Noah for building this ark.
As he worked each day until it was dark,
They laughed and asked him, "Why on dry land?
This Earth will not be destroyed by God's hand."

Only his family would go through the door,
And animals of each kind; there were two or more.
Because eight people had faith to believe,
A new life is what they would receive.

The whole of mankind was washed away forevermore
When out of the floodgates the rain did pour.
As the rain fell, forty days and forty nights,
God turned His head, hid the Earth from His sight.

As the land dried up, a rainbow appeared,
And once again, the Lord would draw near
To those who believed in that open door
That offered hope *before* the rain did pour.

We can still choose to go through that open door,
Or we can choose to just simply ignore.
The Lord Jesus *is* that open door
To the ark that carries us safely ashore.

And after His hand closes the door,
It will be locked forevermore.
The chance to go through will be lost.
Eternal life in heaven is the cost.

Like Noah who entered through that door,
If you believe that Jesus is that door,
You will be saved through Christ's blood,
Just as Noah was saved through the flood.

From God's Own Word

"I am the door: by me, if any man enter in,
he shall be saved" (John 10:9 KJV).

The Fire Escape

I heard Ben say something on Sunday while I was in church.

It set the stage for my mind to begin an interesting search.

I can't remember for sure what he was talking about,

But I knew instantly—there was a poem trying to come out.

I can recall that he talked about escaping the fire,

And it made me think of a situation which could be dire.

If we were in a building that was burning a deadly flame,

We'd just want to get out with no concern for the fire's blame.

It wouldn't matter right then who or what started the blaze.

Our only thought would be how to survive the flames and haze.

In an effort to avoid danger to our lungs, or a bruise or scrape,

We would surely be looking for the closest way to escape!

Suppose someone had warned us of the impending threat,

But we didn't see the flames so thought there was nothing to fret.

Be mindful of the warning of the eternal fiery lake.

If we ignore the warning, we will suffer. Make no mistake.

For God warned us of the day when Christ

will return to judge the world.

He will open the gates of hell, and the scoffers will be hurled.

Or we can trust that the instant Jesus died, God tore the drape

And opened the way to escape the flames: Christ is the fire escape.

From God's Own Word

"We must pay more careful attention, therefore, to what we have heard, so that we do not drift away. For if the message spoken by angels was binding, and every violation and disobedience received its just punishment, how shall we escape if we ignore such a great salvation" (Hebrews 2:1–3)?

The Gate

I tell you the truth, if you come in the sheep pen
Some other way than through Me, if you come in,
You are a thief and a robber and have to leave.
You can only come in through Me—if you believe.

"I tell you the truth, the man who does not
enter the sheep pen by the gate,
but climbs in by some other way, is a thief and a robber"
(John 10:1).

I tell you the truth, I am the gate for the sheep.
I am the gate. All who believe will not weep.
For all who enter through Me, I will save.
They will come and go, but never to the grave.

Therefore, Jesus said again, "I tell you the truth,
I am the gate for the sheep"
(John 10:7).

I am the Good Shepherd. I lay down My life
For all who believe. I give rest from their strife.
I defend My sheep and watch over them
During attacks of madness and mayhem.

"I am the Good Shepherd.
The Good Shepherd lays down His life for the sheep"
(John 10:11).

I am the Good Shepherd, I know my sheep.
And they know Me by the ways that I keep.
They follow My ways, and they know My voice.
They're in My flock if they've made *that* choice.

"I am the Good Shepherd; I know my sheep and my sheep
know me, just as the Father knows me and
I know the Father" (John 10:14).

I lay down my life for these sheep of Mine,
All who have entered through the gate divine.
I know the reason that My Father loves Me;
I lay down My life—for the sheep to be free.

"And I lay down my life for the sheep" (John 10:14).

The Free Ticket

I am going on a trip to a faraway land.
The Lord paid for my ticket with a nail through each hand.
And with the nail that goes through both of His feet,
He has reserved for me a guaranteed seat.

He promised me that He would come and take me away
To the place where He resides each and every day,
The place where all creation worships Him on His throne.
But I must trust in Him. I can't get there on my own.

He said, In my Father's house, there are many rooms:
I will come and take you to be with Me, your Bridegroom.
I am going there to prepare a place for you.
I surely would have told you if this were not true.

He said, You know the way to the place I go.
You can get there for free—with nothing to owe.
But to see this kingdom, you must be born again.
You must be born of God to become a citizen.

Yes, indeed, I'm going on a trip to Paradise!
The Lord has paid for my ticket with His sacrifice.
I thank you, Lord Jesus, for Your love, mercy, and grace,
Which bought and paid for my ticket to come to Your place.

If you would like to take this trip that's completely free,
Just believe He paid the price when He was nailed to the tree.
I am the way and the truth and the life, He said;
No one comes to God except through My blood that was shed.

From God's Own Word

"Do not let your hearts be troubled. Trust in God; trust also in Me. In My Father's house are many rooms; if it were not so, I would have told you. I am going there to prepare a place for you. And if I go and prepare a place for you, I will come back and take you to be with me that you may also be where I am. You know the way to the place where I am going" (John 14:1–4).

The Blanket

I woke up this morning with this picture story in my mind.
It's about a middle-aged lady who was gentle and kind.
I don't know the exact reason why she began her humble search,
But this tale begins one Sunday morning while she was in church.

She needed peace and comfort—the kind promised in the Lord's Word,
And she was trying to understand the promise about which she had heard.
She couldn't grasp the concept. To her, it was all just a blur.
So she asked the preacher if he would please explain it to her.

She asked him, "Why do we have all of this pain, death, and disease,
And how can a Comforter put our weary hearts and souls at ease?
Why must good people experience chaos and disarray,
And why doesn't God just take all this pain and suffering away?"

He replied, "This is not the world God promised would be secure.
He told us that in this world we will have many troubles to endure."
The Lord said, But take heart! I have overcome this earthly sphere.
Do not let your hearts be troubled; trust in God when you have fear.

"The Lord is our Comforter in the midst of gloom and despair,
The way a blanket keeps us warm without removing the cold air.
While He never promised to remove our painful trials and tests,
He does vow that if we come to Him, He will give our souls rest."

The next week, the woman came to church with unusual style.
She was excited and smiling as she was coming up the aisle.
She was shouting, "I've got the blanket. I finally understand.
The Lord comforts us with peace while we live in this troubled land."

From God's Own Word

"For the Lord comforts His people and will have compassion on His afflicted ones" (Isaiah 49:13).

The Vine So True

These are words of the Lord: I am the true Vine.
My Father is the gardener, holy and divine.
My followers are the branches that bear My fruit.
A branch with no vine is sure to be destitute.

For every branch that bears fruit, the Father will prune
So it can bear more fruit. He will finely attune.
If you remain in Me, I will remain in you.
There will be nothing on Earth that you cannot do.

If anyone does not remain in Me,
They will be thrown away like useless debris.
Apart from Me, there is nothing you can do.
Remain in Me, and My words will remain in you.

I love you just as My Father has loved Me.
And I have told you these things so that you might see
That My joy will be in you—that it never ends.
For I no longer call you servants, but friends.

This is what I say to all those who are Mine.
Now you have heard it through the only true Vine.
To all—sister, brother, father, and mother—
I say, "This is my command: Love each other."

From God's Own Word

"I am the vine; you are the branches. If a man remains in Me and I remain in him, he will bear much fruit; apart from Me you can do nothing" (John 15:5).

The Perfect Gentleman

He is my source of faith and hope. I trust Him above all.
He is the love that lifts me when I'm discouraged or I fall.
He always opens doors for me and closes those behind.
He is polite. He never speaks cruel words of any kind.

He never brags about Himself, nor is He ever late.
He'll have nothing to do with envy, lies, prejudice, or hate.
He gives me His arm and holds the umbrella when life's rain pours.
He helps with my coat in life's cold and cools me when its fire roars.

When I cry, He's ready with a handkerchief to dry my tears.
He surrounds me when I'm afraid—to relieve my fears.
When my heart is broken, He stays with me until it's healed.
In fact, He never leaves me—a promise He Himself sealed.

He carries all of my bags, especially those with extra weight.
Whenever I get lost, He guides me and sets my path straight.
He forgives me and helps me whenever I cause disarray
Or when I am rebellious and try to do things my own way.

He always treats me with respect, dignity, and kindness.
He holds a lamp for me so I don't stumble in my blindness.
He keeps me company so I never have to feel alone.
I can truly say that He's the best friend I have ever known.

He is always a perfect gentleman, patient as can be.
He would never demand my love nor force His love on me.
I will boast of Him and His grace—until I have no more breath—
Of Him who died to pay my debt and save me from certain death.

From God's Own Word

"And now these three remain: faith, hope, and love. But the greatest of these is love" (1 Corinthians 13:13).

"Let him who boasts boast in the Lord" (1 Corinthians 1:31).

Section Seven

The Garden

The Dying Rose

I came across a certain Rose one warm summer day.
Not just any rose, this one was withering away.
I envied the beauty of this rose, of its demise,
Of its return to its Maker in the divine skies.

I then wrote a poem about the Lord's bouquet
And the beauty of our flowers when fading away—
How each one is perfect, for each there is a reason,
And how each comes with purpose in its own season.

Two weeks later, I picked up 'Maya Angelou's' poetry book.
The first thing I read gave me a whole new outlook.
Her words said, I once met a lady poet who had seen
The beauty of a dying rose and what it could mean.

She said that a falling leaf could stir her and that a dying rose
Would make her write day and night a most rewarding prose.
Not till I read her words did I think I had a prayer
To think of myself as a poet—I wouldn't dare.

When I read her poem, it was as if the Son warmed my heart.
I thought she spoke of me, it was my poetic jump-start.
Because of Maya's poem, I found a purpose in the Lord
And the faith to accept this most undeserving reward.

From God's Own Word

Each one should use whatever gift he has received to serve others, faithfully administering God's grace in its various forms. If anyone speaks, he should do it as one speaking the very words of God. If anyone serves, he should do it with the strength God provides, so that in all things God may be praised through Jesus Christ. To Him be the glory and the power for ever and ever. Amen. (1 Peter 4:10–11)

The Lord's Bouquet

The life of a flower starts as just a seed
With its beauty inside, soon to be revealed, indeed.
First, the seed must die—the seed that has been sown—
Before the beauty of the flower can be shown.

When the bud appears and each petal is unfurled,
Its beauty and grace will be revealed to the world.
It waits patiently for the exact moment in time
For its glory and splendor to burst forth and shine.

It unfolds gracefully and gently—without rest—
Until perfection is achieved and it's at its best.
Its beauty is unmatched, even as it fades away
For its returning to its Maker, day by day.

Even when a bud withers before it can bloom,
It has not left without leaving a sweet perfume.
Each flower is different in color and in size,
And each one is beautiful in the Lord's eyes.

Because each seed is planted for a unique reason,
It won't return to God before its proper season.
For each seed is planted to bring glory to the Lord.
In every petal, we can see the promise of His Word.

The Lord is arranging a bouquet of His own.
He has a special place for each seed that is sown.
He picks new buds to full blooms to complete His bouquet
But never takes one before its appointed day.

From God's Own Word

"But someone may ask, 'How are the dead raised? With what kind of body will they come?' How foolish! What you sow does not come to life unless it dies. When you sow, you do not plant the body that will be, but just a seed" (1 Corinthians 15:35–36).

The Red Rose

I've been thinking all day long about our treasured Rose.
It's her birthday today; I wonder if she knows.
And because I'm not sure if she can hear what I say,
I asked the Lord to please tell her, "Happy birthday."

I've been thinking about the way that she died,
With all her loved ones surrounding her bedside.
Wasting away, with only her place in heaven left to claim,
Every single minute was filled with intense pain.

I've been thinking about the special day she was born.
An infant—as fresh and new as the dew in the morn.
We weren't there that day to witness her cherished birth,
But we were there the day when her spirit left the Earth.

I've been thinking about how I had prayed to Jesus
To please let our Rosie stay a while longer with us.
I wasn't sure if she had accepted Him just yet,
If she had ever thanked Him for paying her sin's debt.

I've been thinking about how the Lord had blessed me
To look past the anguish, how He allowed me to see
That with each passing day, as Momma withered away,
I was sure she was returning to the Father, Yahweh.

I've been thinking: Like a rare flower was our prized Rose,
A bud with its beauty wrapped tight, waiting for its disclose,
Placed on top of a stem with its thorns and petaled crown,
Then rising closer to heaven as each petal fell down.

I've been thinking about another rose, this one red,
Rising closer to heaven with each drop of blood shed.
Nailed to a stake with wicked thorns as His royal crown,
Dying to restore the petals that have fallen down.

I've been thinking the beauty is this: He rose from the dead,
He died for us, and then He rose on the third day, just like He said.
If you confess "Jesus is Lord" and that through His death He forgave,
And if you believe that God raised Him, you'll never see the grave.

From God's Own Word

"That Christ died for our sins according to the Scriptures, that He was buried, that He was raised on the third day according to the Scriptures" (1 Corinthians 15:3–4).

A Sonflower

Faith is trusting God with the seed sown in the darkness of doubt,
Knowing He'll use our tears, with His light, to grow a worthy sprout.
It's believing He will nourish the dried seed planted in gloom,
To form roots in the deep dark that will sprout a glorious bloom.

A seed is just a dried cell until it's planted in the earth.
Only when it's buried in darkness will we see its true worth.
Like the seed that thrives with dirt, water, and the light of the sun,
We, too, can grow from our tears and the light of hope from the Son.

Just as a seed can't see its beauty when it's first sown in the spring,
We can't see the beauty that our tears
planted in darkness will bring.
So, like the dormant seed planted in the darkness of the soil,
Trust the Lord to bring forth a "Sonflower" from your tearful toil.

From God's Own Word

"Those who sow in tears will reap with songs of joy. He who goes out weeping, carrying seed to sow, will return with songs of joy, carrying sheaves with him" (Psalms 126:5–6).

"Many are asking, 'Who can show us any good?' Let the light of your face shine upon us, O Lord. You have filled my heart with greater joy" (Psalms 4:6–7).

The Voice of Spring

I am thinking about a prayer I heard in church yesterday.

A woman thanked God for the warm, clear day He had sent our way.

I thought of the hope that the flowers and singing birds bring,

And of how the warm sunshine and green
grass are sure signs it's spring.

When she spoke of this return of life being inside and out,

I thought of how our new life in Jesus is like a new sprout

And of how springtime is the perfect time of year to rejoice,

To recall His rising while the birds and flowers raise their voice.

It is no accident that after the long, cold winter gloom,

The birds and flowers sing praise songs as new life begins to bloom.

For just as the frost could not keep this life from being reborn,

Death couldn't keep the Lord Jesus from rising up the third morn.

Through His victory over death, we have spiritual rebirth

And we are reminded of our new life—each spring—here on Earth.

Like the voice of spring that sings to worship God's supreme glory,

The angels rejoice when even *one* believes the Cross story.

God promised us eternal life with the rising of His Son.

We are reminded of His vow each day with the rising sun.

And if you listen closely, the voices of angels can be heard

When you believe the case for Christ according to God's Word.

From God's Own Word

See! The winter is past; the rains are over and gone.
Flowers appear on the Earth; the season of singing has come,
the cooing of doves is heard in our land.
The fig tree forms its early fruit;
the blossoming vines spread their fragrance.
(Song of Songs 2:11–13)

"I tell you the truth, he who believes has everlasting life" (John 6:47).

Springtime

Small buds line each branch. There's a faint
green haze across the lawns.

Sunshine warms the cool morning air as
the light of a new day dawns.

The fragrance of blossoms and flowers fills the air with sweetness,

And the birds are singing as they build their
nests with zest and neatness.

The farmers are planting the seeds of
their crops all in a straight row.

They mix the soil and fertilizer with water to make them grow.

The fruit trees are forming their fruit, and
the vines begin their climb.

With each day longer than the last, it's plain to see it's springtime.

With the springtime, I am reminded of my new life with Christ.

I was dead to sin until I believed that He was sacrificed,

That through the death of His earthly body I've been made alive,

And it's in the power of His triumph over sin where I thrive.

I'm reconciled to God through His Son—He's worthy to be praised!

And, just as Jesus was raised from the dead, I have also been raised.

The winter is past; now I flourish in God's holy Sonlight.

I now have peace with God; I'm presented as holy in His sight.

I was dead in sin. I was frozen in the dirt of the Earth.

Then, Jesus's light warmed me, He thawed
me out and gave me a new birth.

With His flesh and blood, I was bought and planted as His daughter.

He's the soil that holds my roots, my life's sustaining food and water.

The Lord is the garden that made me sprout. He causes new growth.

He raised me up as a new creation according to His oath.

Like the seed that's planted in dirt and is raised a fragrant flower,

I was buried with Him through baptism
and then raised by His power.

From God's Own Word

"For as the soil makes the sprout come up and a garden causes seeds to grow, so the Sovereign Lord will make righteousness and praise spring up before all nations" (Isaiah 61:11).

"We were therefore buried with Him through baptism into death in order that, just as Christ was raised from the dead through the glory of the Father, we too may live a new life" (Romans 6:4).

Gray to Purple

While riding on the motorcycle one gorgeous spring day,

I saw some rocky bluffs. The surface was gray, hard, and rough.

But somehow some pretty purple flowers had found their way

Through a tiny crack in the stone that seemed so hard and tough.

Then we passed a farmer's field filled with dirt and winter's gray,

With a patch of purple flowers springing up through the earth.

How I love springtime and the picture its colors portray:

That after a long winter, there is still hope for new birth.

I saw a purple flower growing through desolate gray.

It was in a photo of volcano ash I had once seen.

It declared that there's always hope, no matter what blows our way.

The promise told is priceless in this image so serene.

Then a lone tree colored with a delicate purple spray

Made me think of the value of this royal color's cast.

It stood among other trees that were still leafless and gray.

All by itself, it offered hope that the winter had passed.

I was then reminded of a loving purple bouquet.

My sister had sent it because she wanted me to know

That it's the strongest color we have when our skies are gray,

Because it's compiled of all the colors in the rainbow.

That leads me to think of yet another purple display.

After Christ was flogged, clothed in purple, and struck in the face,

He was crowned with thorns, and then
the King was crucified that day.

He rose from death so gray, which gives
us hope for life—through grace.

From God's Own Word

"Then Pilate took Jesus and had Him flogged. The soldiers twisted together a crown of thorns and put it on His head. They clothed Him in a purple robe and went up to Him again and again, saying, 'Hail, King of the Jews!' and they struck Him in the face" (John 19:1–3).

"We believe it is through the grace of our Lord Jesus that we are saved" (Acts 15:11).

Growing Faith and Hope

If God allows a difficult growing season,
Then rest assured—He has a very good reason.
Because He has no accidents, no oversights.
So, if He has approved suffering, then it must be right.

We must trust Him during times of hardship and pain,
Even though we can see nothing from which we can gain.
It takes faith when we plant a seed in a field
To believe that we will harvest a worthy yield.

We can't see the hardy and useful plant inside
Unless we believe enough to plant its dry seed outside.
Without faith, we won't take the time to nurture and care
For a dried-up seed planted in the dirt so bare.

There are many reasons why the Lord allows these times,
So we must persevere through harsh and evil crimes.
Though it seems there can be no real sensible grounds,
We have to trust His love and comfort, which abounds.

God is growing faith and hope for all who persevere,
If we trust Him to water that seed with each tear.
He's promised to comfort us when we are down-and-out.
If He has planted a seed, He's sure to make it sprout.

From God's Own Word

"For you know that when your faith is tested, your endurance
has a chance to grow. So let it grow" (James 1:3–4).

"Those who plant in tears will harvest with shouts of joy.
They weep as they go to plant their seed, but they sing
as they return with the harvest" (Psalms 126:5–6).

What He Needs

No one has ever asked him what he needs.
No one has ever planted worthy seeds.
No one gave him anything but loathing and doubt.
No one gave him what worthy seeds need to sprout.

Try to ask him what he thinks might be his needs.
Try to plant in him much-needed worthy seeds.
Try to plant confidence instead of self-doubt.
Try to give time for the precious seeds to sprout.

Ask him what he needs to feel safe and secure.
Ask him what it would take to help him endure.
Ask him what he needs to love himself and care.
Ask him what he thinks his needs are—if you dare.

We can say what will lift his spirit, not suppress.
We can encourage him in self-worth and success.
We can't accept it for him; it is his own choice.
We can, however, tell of God's love with our voice.

What he needs is to feel that someone loves and cares.
What he needs is to know God hears all his prayers.
What he needs to know is that human beings are weak.
What he needs to know is that God is the parent he seeks.

Even a seed that's planted in unhealthy soil,
Its only cares being doubt, neglect, and turmoil,
Can become well again with a will to survive
If we nourish it with the love it needs to thrive.

From God's Own Word

"So encourage each other and build each other up" (1 Thessalonians 5:11).

"Tell God what you need, and thank Him for all He has done" (Philippians 4:6).

Section Eight

The Gift

Gifts from All These Men

I'd like for you to meet the most important men in my life.

There's Chris and Jeff, my sons, and "lucky" Larry has me for a wife.

Marvin's dad, Bernie's dad-in-law—there's
Kenny and my brother Kirk.

They all have earned their living doing
some sort of construction work.

I have been thinking about how interesting it is to me

That all these men are able to work with wood—to some degree.

And, though some enjoy it more than others, it's the work they chose

To provide for themselves and their family food, shelter, and clothes.

Kirk can paint, but wood cabinets are what
he would much rather build.

And Dad can build with wood, although
painting it is where he's most skilled.

All these men have built special things for
me with wood, hammer, and nails,

Like a desk, shelves, tables, stools, homes,
and decks with fancy handrails.

I will treasure each one's toil for me until my dying day,

Then they'll be in heaven with me, though on Earth they will decay.

Which leads me to the *greatest* man in my life—Jesus, my Lord.

While living on Earth, He was also skilled
with nail, hammer, and board.

While I prize these gifts from all these men,
I cherish the Lord's gift more.

His was made with nails, hammer, wood, His
flesh, and *my* sins that He bore.

With the pure blood that poured from His
wounds and the pain He endured,

All my debts were *paid in full,* and my salvation was secured.

Lord, thank you for the gift of grace and faith that You built for me,

For taking *all* my sins with their code and nailing them to the tree.

The gift of pardon is in Your blood—for each precious drop that fell

Was filled with Your grace, which, through
faith, redeems us from hell.

From God's Own Word

"He Himself bore our sins in His body on the tree, so
that we might die to sins and live for righteousness; by
His wounds you have been healed" (1 Peter 2:24).

"He forgave us all our sins, having canceled the written code,
with its regulations, that was against us and that stood opposed
to us; He took it away, nailing it to the cross" (Colossians 2:13–14).

God's Free Gift

We teach our children about the miracles of Santa Claus,
But when it comes to teaching them about Jesus, there is pause.
So, then, when someone tells them about God's almighty power,
They simply won't let themselves be fooled again—so they cower.

Sometimes, it takes a whole lifetime to get past this childhood sham
And be able to put faith and trust in God's holy Lamb.
I'm asking you to be aware of this confusion and fact,
So we can keep our children's grasp of what's truth and lie intact.

Please take the time to think about this and find a noble way
To celebrate the birth of Christ without a huge price to pay.
We can't expect to teach our kids not to fib—don't tell a lie—
If we convince them of Santa while looking them in the eye.

I said it before and I say it now again: Santa Claus is a lie.
Santa cannot save us, or our precious children, when we die.
But rather it is Jesus who came from heaven to save us.
To believe anything else is eternally dangerous.

That is what Christmastime is, a time to recognize Christ's birth,
God in the flesh coming to dwell with us on this broken Earth.
We should use the lessons learned about taking gifts and giving
To accept God's free gift so that when we die, we won't stop living.

Whatever you choose to tell them, please tell them of God's free gift.
Let them come to Jesus, trusting that He will not send them adrift.
This promise is also for you who will put your faith in Him.,
Trust Him with childlike faith and He'll save you from eternal grim.

From God's Own Word

"The free gift of God is eternal life through
Christ Jesus our Lord" (Romans 6:23).

"God's free gift leads to our being made right with God,
even though we are guilty of many sins" (Romans 5:16).

The Real Gift

What if we told our children the truth about the Christmas season,

That it's not Santa Claus, but Jesus's birth, that is the real reason?

What if we told them that the real gift is
wrapped in Christ Jesus's birth,

That Immanuel, "God is with us," came from heaven to live on Earth.

It's a time to honor Jesus's birthday, not just get presents—

A special time of year to acknowledge the gift of God's presence.

We could still make it seem magical without telling them a lie.

After all, it's Jesus, not Santa, who will save them when they die.

It would relieve holiday despair when Santa can't provide,

And we might even hear fewer reports of holiday suicide.

Think of how it could bless those who feel lonely during the holidays

If they knew they were never alone, that their Savior never strays?

"But it's not fair," some might say; "the
children won't get to have their fun."
The children would know no difference if we hadn't let it begin.

It's what we teach them when they're babies.
It starts purely for our own joy.
We just want to see the surprise in their eyes with each opened toy.

But is it worth it to possibly lose their trust and faith in us,

Having to wonder why they doubt us when we talk about Jesus?

When I think of lies I told my children in the name of make-believe

And recall their heartbreak upon hearing the
truth, it makes my heart grieve.

If we'd start the tradition with the truth and maybe a grand feast,

The children could still have fun without
feeling deceived and fleeced.

We're able to find ways to have magical fun for their birthday,

So why not for Jesus's birthday find a fun that does not betray?

They could learn the secret of giving and how it should give us joy.

But they would learn this with truth, not
a lie meant to seek and destroy.

For, you see, it's no accident, it is no joke to be told,

That if you move the n in *Santa,* you get the *Satan* of old.

I'm not saying not to give your children
gifts or give up their surprise.

What I'm saying is to tell them the truth
and see real love in their eyes.

They can learn about giving through real stories like that of St. Nick,

And they will embrace the gift of Jesus without suspecting a trick.

Children will still have their imaginations at work while they play,

And we won't worry about popping their magic bubble someday.

We won't be the first one in their lives to teach them about pretense,

Assuring them of lies that even to some four-
year-olds don't make sense.

From God's Own Word

"For the wages of sin is death, but the free gift of God is eternal life through Christ Jesus our Lord" (Romans 6:23).

"Stop deceiving yourselves. If you think you are wise by this world's standards, you need to become a fool to be truly wise" (1 Corinthians 4:18).

Wise Men

It was in the days of Caesar Augustus.
He issued a decree for a census.
This new law turned everything upside down,
For each had to register in his or her own town.

So Joseph went to the town of Bethlehem.
Mary went, too; she was pledged to marry him.
She was a virgin, expecting her first child
At the same time the census was to be filed.

While they were there, Mary gave birth to a son.
Not just *any* son, He was God's Holy One.
She wrapped Him in bands of cloth to keep Him warm
And placed Him in a manger, safe from all harm.

She gave her baby boy the name of Jesus,
Which also means *Immanuel,* "God with us."
All this took place to fulfill what God had said—
That a King would be born in a humble shed.

There were shepherds living in the fields nearby,
Keeping watch over their flocks beneath the night sky.
An angel of the Lord appeared to them
And told them of the child born in Bethlehem.

So they hurried to seek Him of whom they had heard,
That this baby Jesus was "the Good Shepherd."
They followed His star, till there in the hay,
They found the Lord Jesus asleep where He lay.

They brought Him gifts and worshiped Him with joy.
The wise men knew—this was not just *any* boy!
Wise men still seek this Savior, Christ the King,
And give Him their hearts as their offering.

From God's Own Word

"You will seek me and find me when you seek me with all your heart" (Jeremiah 29:13).

If I Only Knew...

If I knew the coming day I might better prepare,
For what The Lord will say to me when I get there.
If I knew the day, I surely wouldn't stall so much,
Nor, would I be using self pity as a crutch.

I 'd sure make better use of my talents and my time,
Even if it meant working a lot of overtime.
If I had to, I would work both day and night,
In order to be sure that everything was just right.

To insure it was complete, I'd stay very busy,
I'd move so fast - all those around me would be dizzy.
Just so I could hear those words coming from the Son:
'Well done, My good and faithful servant, Well done.'

I'd be more careful about what I say to others,
And bid help to widows, orphans, and single mothers,
I would take the blame for the choices that I've made,
Then thank The Lord Jesus for the price that He paid.

I would repent of my sins, and ask Him to forgive,
Then turn away from them all with a new way to live.
I'd share all I have, and make straight paths for Him too,
To prepare the way for The Lord, If I Only Knew.

But, since I don't know the times or dates set by God,
I don't think I'll rely on this shaky ground I trod.
I think I shall start right now, in case He comes today,
So I won't have to look Him in the eyes and say;

Lord, I am sorry that my work is not finished yet,
For my lax tongue, and not helping with the poor's debt.
I'm sorry for all the waste, and what I never shared.
Lord, if I Only Knew...
I surely would have chosen to be more prepared

From God's Own Word

Now concerning how and when all this will
happen, dear brothers and sisters,
we don't really need to write you. For you know
quite well that the day of the Lord's
return will come unexpectedly, like a thief in
the night. When people are saying,
"Everything is peaceful and secure," then
disaster will fall on them as suddenly as
a pregnant woman's labor pains begin. And
then there will be no escape.
1 Thessalonians 5:1-3

Please Come In

Will you have room should Jesus knock tonight,

Then, be wise and follow His divine starlight?

Or, will you say He must go out in the barn,

That you have no place where He can be born?

Or, will you say, Oh Jesus please come in.

Be born in my heart and let new life begin.

I unlock and open wide my hearts' door,

For you to come live with me forevermore.

From God's Own Word

After Jesus was born in Bethlehem in Judea, during the time of
King Herod, Magi from the east came to Jerusalem and asked,
"Where is the one who has been born king of
the Jews? We saw His star in the east
and have come to worship Him."
Matthew 2:1-2

In reply Jesus declared,
"I tell you the truth, no one can see the kingdom
of God unless he is born again."
John 3:3

I Thank-You Lord

I thank-you Lord Jesus for all your deeds,
For always providing for my needs.
Your ways [forever] stay righteous and true,
I am so thankful for You being You.

I thank-you Lord for all that you have done,
And for all the things that are still to come.
I know that you use 'all' things for the good
Of those who love you, You promised you would.

I thank-you Lord for your blessings of love
From family and friends, and You up above.
Without love, I would have no faith or hope,
[Love] is the power that helps me to cope.

I thank-you Lord for always hearing me
When I call out to you on bended knee.
What a blessing to know you heard my need
And, to be certain You will provide indeed!

I thank-you Lord on this Thanksgiving Day
For all the gifts that you have sent my way.
But, the one gift - that I'm most thankful for;
Giving Your life to open Heaven's door.

From God's Own Word

You are my God, and I will give you thanks;
you are my God, and I will exalt you.
Give thanks to The Lord, for He is good;
His love endures forever.
Psalm 118:28-29

Section Nine

Our Choices

The Choice

A friend once told me that he wished it could be
As easy as choosing door one, two, or three.
I told him, "The choice *can* be made with such ease
If you just listen to the facts, which are these."

Door Number One
Jesus is God, who was crucified for us.
He paid our debt completely. Thank you, Lord Jesus.
On the third day, He rose from the dead, from His grave,
To fulfill His promise: Our souls He will save.

Door Number Two
We can believe in someone or something else,
With no hope of release from our prison cells.
No escape from our guilt, the torture within.
No promise of life with forgiveness of sin.

Door Number Three
We can *think* there's no afterlife, or maybe worse.
We keep coming back on some immortal course.
We have no hope that hardship or pain will ever cease,
And no promise for life with eternal peace.

We make our own choices; that is free will.
We can believe in the One whose blood did spill
Or believe in the doors that have no promise
And spend our eternity in the abyss.

Think carefully about the door that you choose.
If you pick the wrong door, you will surely lose
Your chance to be saved by the Spirit's rebirth.
You can't change your mind after you leave this earth.

From God's Own Word

"Salvation is found in no one else, for there is no other name under heaven given to men by which we must be saved" (Acts 4:12).

Redemption or Rejection

Whether you call it a cross, stake, or tree,
On that particular day, there were three.
Three men were to die on their cross that day,
But only two were guilty of crimes to pay.

They were led out to the place called the Skull.
There, they would be hung as a spectacle.
We know two were robbers, guilty of theft.
One would hang on the right; the other, on the left.

Jesus was guilty of nothing, and yet
He would hang in the center to pay our debt.
He asked the Father to forgive them all.
"They know not what they do," after all.

The people, watching, mocked and sneered at Him.
"Let Him save Himself, if it's truly Him.
If He's *the Son of God, the chosen one,*
Then He will come down before it is done."

One of the criminals hurled insults at Him.
He did not believe that Christ could remove sin.
But the other said, "Our punishment is just,
But this man is innocent. In Him I trust."

Then he said, "Jesus, remember me,
When You come into the kingdom of Thee."
Jesus answered him, "I tell you no lies;
Today you'll be with Me in Paradise."

There were three crosses on that faithful day.
In which will you place your trust today?
If you choose the cross of repentance now,
Then you'll receive the cross of redemption, *His* vow.

If you choose the cross of rejection, then woe;
I don't need to tell you where you will go.
Eternal torment is what you'll receive,
All because you flat-out refused to believe!

From God's Own Word

"For my Father's will is that everyone who looks to the Son
and believes in Him *shall* have eternal life, and I *will* raise
him up at the last day" (John 6:40, emphasis added).

"I told you that you would die in your sins; if you do not believe that I
am the one I claim to be, you will indeed die in your sins" (John 8:24).

From God's Own Word

"But who do you say I am?" (Mark 8:29)
"I am the resurrection and the life. Anyone who believes
in me will live, even after dying. Everyone who lives in
me and believes in me will never die." (John 11:25-26)

Simply Stated

Evolution states that we humans could be
Nothing more than a glorified monkey,
That we have evolved from a long line of apes.
We're educated chimps with an upright traipse.

The big bang theory states some big, huge blowout.
It would have been a destructive blast, no doubt.
That would make humans the result of a mess,
With a heritage of havoc to possess.

Creation states that human beings were made
In the image of God when His hand was laid
Upon the earth as He breathed the breath of life.
This began mankind:, Adam and, then, Eve, his wife.

While the world *will* evolve every second today
And a "big bang" might explain our destructive way,
To be made in the image of God seems, to me,
Much better than being a glorified monkey!

While science can explain how the earth keeps turning,
And, while it might tell us how the stars keep burning,
It can't tell us how the human heart keeps yearning,
Nor, where we came from and to where we're returning.

From God's Own Word

"Then God said, 'Let us make man in our own image, and let them rule over the fish of the sea and the birds of the air, over the livestock, over all the earth, and over all the creatures that move along the ground.' So God created man in His own image, in the image of God He created him male and female He created them" (Genesis 1:26–27).

Angels

Don't deny the credit due to those who help you in any way.

Give them acknowledgement for giving you hope for a better day.

Give them the thank-you they deserve, which you can surely afford.

But most of all, give all the praise, honor, and glory to the Lord.

For it's the Lord who sends others in His
place to help answer prayers.

They are called His angels, those He sends
to relieve worries and cares.

From God's Own Word

"Keep on loving each other as brothers and sisters. Don't forget to show hospitality to strangers, for some who have done this have entertained angels without realizing it" (Hebrews 13:1–2)!

Partial definitions of Angel from The Free Dictionary by Farlex. (online dictionary)

Angel (ān'jel) n.

1. a typically benevolent celestial being that acts as an intermediary between heaven and earth.
2. a representation of such a being.
3. angels in Christianity—the last of the nine orders of angels in medieval angelology.
4. a guardian spirit or guiding influence.
5.
   a. a kind and lovable person.
   b. one who manifests goodness, purity, and selflessness.

Buried Treasure

Won't you come over here and sit down next to me?
I'll tell you of a treasure that's completely free.
It's worth is more than all of the earth's jewels so fine,
And it's *light* is brighter than the midday sunshine.

It cannot be bought or sold for any amount.
Not even the most precious stones can surmount.
We won't find it by climbing the highest of highs
Or by searching the world with spacecraft in the skies.

We won't find it buried in the deepest of seas,
And it can't be captured with any forceful seize.
There is no scale or standard rule that can measure
The worthiness of this long-lost buried treasure.

It can't be found in any piece of priceless art,
But it can be found by searching no further than your heart.
You see, we've possessed this treasure since long ago,
But we didn't recognize its heavenly glow.

And it's still there, buried deep beneath all our *stuff,*
Under all the *things* that will never be enough.
You will realize this truth while searching on your quest.
You'll find your buried treasure in your treasure chest.

From God's Own Word

"But we have this treasure in jars of clay" (2 Corinthians 4:7).

"But you know him, for he lives with you
and will be in you" (John 14:17).

Your Best Suit

I read a wise quote recently that I would like to share.

It said this: "Grandma always said, 'Words
are the clothes our thoughts wear.

It's no wonder that the tabloid papers and gossip mags

Are usually referred to as trash and/or filthy rags.'"

So we would all do well to keep this quote fresh in our mind,

To think twice before we speak and say only what is kind.

For it takes just a split second to slice open a heart,

And sometimes even a lifetime can't mend what's torn apart.

He who guards his lips and puts a hold on his tongue is wise.

With no control, our tongues can be the source of our demise.

For it takes just a spark to set a great forest on fire

And just a moment to reveal our thoughts' complete attire.

What will your thoughts wear today? How
will you dress up each word?

Will it be drab and dirty rags that are downright absurd?

Or will you choose something nice, a pleasant and loving speech,

Clothes that encourage peace, hope, and
faith, which strengthen and teach?

Pleasant words are sweet to the soul and healing to the bones,

And a person's thoughts are judged by the wardrobe that she owns.

So be careful today when choosing the
clothes your thoughts will wear:

Select your best suit, and dress your
thoughts with distinguished flair.

From God's Own Word

"When words are many, sin is not absent, but he who holds his tongue is wise" (Proverbs 10:19).

"He who guards his lips guards his life, but he who speaks rashly will come to ruin" (Proverbs 13:3).

Baggage

I have been thinking about the baggage we carry around.

We drag so much with us—it seems we're international-bound.

We have all these bags filled with this and
that—mostly useless stuff—

And the only thing all this weight does is make us huff and puff.

We just can't use most of the contents of these oppressive bags.

Even the clothing we pack will soon turn to meaningless rags.

We've packed useless inanimate objects—symbols of our pride—

Like machinery that only gives us but a moment's ride.

Some of the bags we lug are filled with barren heartaches and pain.

There's absolutely nothing left in them that has worth or brings gain.

If we had known just how much these painful
scars would come to weigh,

Would we have thrown them out long ago—
somewhere along the way?

We have bags and bags that embody all of our mistakes and guilt,

While others hold regrets, and needless shame is filled to the hilt.

We even have suitcases filled with nothing but thin air

Waiting for us to start packing in another useless care.

What are we to do with baggage that has no purpose to serve?

How do we decide what to unpack and what we should reserve?

If we ask the Lord, He will help carry our cumbersome freight.

He'll discard what is useless to relieve us of excess weight.

From God's Own Word

"Praise be to the Lord, to God our Savior, who daily bears our burdens" (Psalms 68:19).

"Come to me, all who are weary and burdened, and I will give you rest. Forgetting what is behind and straining toward what is ahead" (Philippians 3:13).

Money

There are those who say, "Of evil, money is the root."
They believe that all evil begins and ends with loot.
But I believe it can be used for the good of man.
If we use it properly, I have faith that it can.

I truly believe that money is like a tool,
But we must use it wisely, not like a fool.
Money can help us to be rich with good deeds.
It can be used to help those with special needs.

Money is a device, just like a gun or a knife.
We can use them to create chaos and strife
Or protection, food, and clothing to enjoy.
But they can be lethal if we use them as a toy.

It's not the money itself that causes upheaval.
Rather, it's the *love of money* that causes evil.
The root of all evil lies in the choices we make—
What we choose to give and the amount that we take.

Peace, faith, and hope are what generosity breed.
Turmoil, gloom, and despair are the results of greed.
I don't believe that money is the root of all evil;
It's our choice to love money that causes upheaval.

The *love of money* can create all kinds of grief.
It will cause us to act no better than a thief.
At times, we'll lie and cheat just to get a little more.
It doesn't matter if we take from the rich or the poor.

The root of all evil is buried deep in our souls.
It tempts and traps us; it destroys our honest goals.
We get lost in harmful desires and plunge into spoil,
And then the fruit of our labor is ruin and turmoil.

Money is a gift from God, to be used in His name.
When we abuse this privilege, we store up shame.
We can't serve both God and money without disaster.
We can only be faithful to one as our Master.

From God's Own Word

"For the *love of money* is a root of all kinds of evil. People who want to get rich fall into temptation and a trap and into many foolish and harmful desires that plunge men into ruin and destruction" (1 Timothy 6:9–10, emphasis added).

"No one can serve two masters. Either he will hate the one and love the other, or he will be devoted to the one and despise the other. You cannot serve both God and money" (Matthew 6:24).

Freedom to Choose

Don't be confused about your calling to be free,
Or you just might end up serving the Enemy.
The Lord made it clear in the Word of Life He gave,
That we make our own choice to whom we shall be a slave.

Christ died to set us free from the power of sin
And to give us strength to fight sin's nature within.
That doesn't mean we have freedom to do just as we please.
That would make us slaves again to sin's chocking squeeze.

The acts of sin's nature can be seen crystal clear
If we look with our heart and listen with our hearts ear.
And if we're living by the Spirit of the Lord,
We'll not gratify desires that create discord.

We'll be able to stand against the Devil's bait
And not get caught in traps of jealousy and hate.
We'd have no fits of rage, envy, or drunkenness,
No dissensions, factions, selfishness, or excess.

We would have no orgies or vile sex that's impure,
No false gods or idols and no witchcraft, for sure.
The fruits of God's Spirit are peace, love, and kindness,
Faith, hope, joy, patience, self-control, and goodness.

So remember, when *you choose* whom you'll serve today,
That Christ died to pay your debt and save you from decay—
Not to give you freedom to do as you desire,
But to live *by His* Words, not those of a liar.

From God's Own Word

"You, my brothers, were called to be free. But do not use your freedom to indulge in the sinful nature" (Galatians 5:13).

"So I say, live by the Spirit, and you will not gratify the desires of the sinful nature" (Galatians 5:16).

Section Ten

Hope in Wartime

The War Within

This world we live in is torn by war.
The Enemy knows right where we are.
All through the day and into the night,
He never lets us out of his sight.

This war was declared a long time ago.
Its goal is to destroy our very soul.
With a different battle every day,
Traps are constantly set in our way.

His strategy is full of lies and deceit.
Our faith and hope are what he wants to defeat.
The jagged arrows shoot right through the heart.
They shred and rip us completely apart.

Drugs and booze are just some of the tools
That he uses to make us his fools.
He is cunning, and he strikes from behind.
We know it's wrong, but he says to never mind.

His schemes are cruel and sometimes vicious.
They strip our dignity away from us.
He knows exactly where it hurts the most.
To weakness, pain, and fear, he is the host.

He wants to win, so he doesn't fight fair.
He uses loneliness and also despair
To bring our esteem down to his level—
To the residing place of the Devil.

In the midst of the battle, we lose our way.
We don't even realize that we've gone astray.
We fall into a trap with a hold so strong
That we can't even tell right from wrong.

When our way is completely confused,
He then begins to blame and accuse.
We lose all our faith and all of our hope.
It takes all we have just to try to cope.

We can't seem to make our hopeless way clear.
We can't see that he is always so near.
The Enemy is just a step away
From our hearts, every minute of the day.

The pit of darkness offers no way out
Of this world full of misery and doubt.
There is no hope for poor, wretched me.
Pain and fear is all there will ever be.

Then a bright light shines from up above.
It shatters the darkness with its love.
Faith, hope, and strength come with it, as well.
It's from the One who delivers from hell.

It guides us back to the path that is right.
An awesome blessing is this heavenly light.
It shines brightly for all those who believe
That faith and hope is the gift they will receive.

We don't ever have to be all alone
While trying to survive in this war zone
If we believe that we have a constant shield
Always in front of us on the battlefield.

He is there, waiting to come to our rescue.
But we have to believe that it is true.
He would fill us with endless faith and hope
If we would just ask Him to help us cope.

When the war is over and it is won,
The Devil *will* be conquered by the Son.
There is no doubt; this much is surely true.
The Lord promised to defend me and you.

Thank you, Lord, for your heavenly light
That guides us back to the path that is right
And away from the ways that are so wrong,
Back in your arms, forever, where we belong.

From God's Own Word

"Finally, be strong in the Lord and in His mighty power. Put on the full armor of God so that you can take your stand against the devil's schemes. For our struggle is not against flesh and blood, but against the rulers, against the authorities, against the powers of this dark world and against the spiritual forces of evil in the heavenly realms" (Ephesians 6:10).

"The weapons we fight with are not the weapons of the world. On the contrary, they have divine power to demolish strongholds" (2 Corinthians 10:4).

The Cesspool

I once had a dream of what seemed like a large cesspool
Filled with every kind of vice that could make one a fool.
Its banks held a thick, foul sludge and was filled to the brim—
An image of how drugs and booze make life dark and grim.

I heard a voice say that this pool was filled with human waste
And to do what I could to clean it up—without haste.
I understood "human waste" not as human feces.
Rather, it meant the wasting of the human species.

I realized instantly who was in this filthy lake.
Even though I could not see them, there was no mistake.
Something had to be done, and it had to be done fast,
To help rescue and recover them from this vile past.

They needed others to help them climb out of this pit
And to help them see they were not just some poor misfits.
In the dream, I knew it was the voice of urgency.
Someone was about to die... it was an emergency.

I awoke from this dream to see a man standing by,
Waiting to help the one who was about to die.
At first, I was startled by the shadow of this man,
But then I realized he was there to say, "Oh yes, you can."

I believe that God always sends us the help that we need,
Someone or something to encourage us to succeed.
To set our feet on solid rock is God's desire,
So He will lift us from our slimy pit of mud and mire.

He'll rescue us from the deep waters before we sink.
He won't let the pit swallow us when we're on the brink.
When we cry, "Come quick to my rescue," He'll turn His ear.
He won't hide His face when we're in trouble; He'll come near.

From God's Own Word

"He lifted me out of the slimy pit, out of the mud and mire; He set my feet on a rock and gave me a place to stand" (Psalms 40:2).

"Do not let the floodwaters engulf me or the depths swallow me up or the pit close its mouth over me. Do not hide your face from your servant; answer me quickly, for I am in trouble. Come near and rescue me" (Psalms 69:15–18).

The Mirror

Suppose we asked the far-famed mirror on the wall
To please reveal the fairest truth—once and for all.
And suppose it replied, "Look deep and we will find
Our truest reflection in the hearts of all humankind."

And what if it said that the truth hardest to accept
Is the thing we find in others who are inept?
Because it's that we see in others that we hate the most,
That we dislike in our own selves—so let us not boast.

I'm not suggesting that we always practice what we hate,
Only that we might think of or feel these things with great weight.
So we must contemplate before judging others' deeds,
Unless we're prepared to harvest our own planted seeds.

From God's Own Word

"Why do you look at the speck of sawdust in your brother's eye and
pay no attention to the plank in your own eye" (Matthew 7:3)?

"You hypocrite, first take the plank out of your own
eye, and then you will see clearly to remove the
speck from your brother's eye" (Matthew 7:5).

Section Eleven

The Fall

The Fall in New York

Larry and I had just returned from a long, fall
weekend with friends in New York City.

We saw many awesome sights while there, and
some of them seemed to be a pity.

We saw little remaining of what the city had
come to be—before the new mayor,

Because he'd cleaned up the town and
restored its beauty, charm, and flair.

Our first stop was Patsy's for an early dinner,
where Beth and I talked with the cook.

When he said he'd been on TV, we were so
impressed that we bought his cookbook!

Then we went to Greenwich Village and
found a nice, cozy house of ale

From where we watched people and ate pizza
while enjoying an evening cocktail.

When we saw the band setting up to play,
we decided we had better move.

We thought their music would be loud and
obnoxious, way out of our groove.

But the band was great; classic rock was
the only music that they played.

Even though we were *too tired* to dance, we
were all glad that we stayed.

We talked about how life has changed us, even
though we swore that it wouldn't,

And about watching our kids change and grow
and do things they really shouldn't.

We spoke of how old we have all gotten and
laughed about our newest ways.

We said, "We can still run with the big dogs,
just not as fast as in our yesterdays."

We left first thing the next morning for
Central Park to take an easy stroll.

We saw unique elm trees and cops riding
horses that were there on patrol.

We saw lots and lots of dogs walking and
playing with their very best friends.
We saw one that *wet* on a man's leather backpack—
and the owner looking for amends.

Then we went to see a play about scoundrels
whose antics were dirty and rotten.
It was quite amusing. I'm sure all their
shenanigans won't soon be forgotten.

Afterward, Beth and I went to Fifth Avenue
to do a little shopping,

While Larry and Tom did what they liked
best: They were off bar-hopping.

As Beth and I were walking, we came across a famous worship place.

It was St. Patrick's, a cathedral with a majestic beauty to embrace.

As we entered inside for a peek (for we surely
could not pass this sight by),

I was so overwhelmed with the Divine
presence that I thought I might cry.

We didn't have much time to see every detail
because we had to meet the men,

But I remembered watching the memorial that was made after 9/11.

Beth told me all that she could as we walked
through this house of worship,

But I'd love to come back and get a closer
look sometime on a future trip.

The next morning, we went to the sight of the 9/11 attack,

Where terror has forever filled our hearts
and memories with billows of black.

There have not yet been any words spoken
to describe what I saw and felt,

Seeing the hole where evil burned so hot that
the strongest of steel would melt.

This is not just a hole in New York where
evil and horror was unfurled,

And it's not just a big hole in the United
States. It's a hole in the world.

It's a wound, not only on the surface of Earth,
but also one that goes so deep

That people all over the world have been
affected by it; many hearts still weep.

While there, I heard a man with a flute play
"Amazing Grace," and I saw a steel cross.

The cross was found in the rubble, a gift
from God in this time of great loss.

The cross reminded me that the Lord is always
with us—even in times of despair—

While the sound of His promise to heal with
"Amazing Grace" filled the air.

Did we know that when we began to ask God to
leave our workplaces, homes, and schools,

We'd have no right to blame Him when evil
men used our planes as deadly tools?

And do we realize yet, through the fall of
each sky-high World Trade Tower,

That we need Him back in our nation to restore
peace with His amazing power?

Our next stop was the Statue of Liberty. She stands tall for all to see.

We the people will stand together in our great country—'tis of Thee.

That the *United States* means exactly what it states—united as one—

One for all and all for one, a country that will be divided by none.

While we were waiting in line, there was a man
who could sing a song about any state.

He was singing for money with a guitar and
rainbow wig... and we took the bait.

Then we met a man who said his cousin lived
in our town, a man of great fame.

But he hadn't seen his cousin since the "watching
young girls in the bathroom" shame.

This man said that he was a singer who
has never left his gospel songs.

He also told me how some people, at times,
will bring up the Southern wrongs.

They will say bad things about white people and
about the killings motivated by race,

But he'll say, "Wait, you can't talk about my
brothers and sisters with such disgrace!"

When they reply, "Your brothers and sisters!?
Your skin is black; theirs is white,"

He says, "But why does it matter so much if
their skin color is dark or light?

We are all brothers and sisters, because we're
all family in our heart and soul."

I believe that this man has enough love and
wisdom to fill that monstrous hole.

I don't know this man's name, only that he
wore a smile and a purple shirt.

And all his belongings sat next to him in a
blue case, and his bed was the dirt.

He said he was coming to St. Louis soon to
record an album with his band.

The Soul Lifters is their name. They sing
gospel music throughout our land.

Some would say this man was not telling the
truth, that his words were a bunch of lies,

That he's a crazy dreamer and a drunkard
with his head up in the skies.

But I enjoyed our visit so much that it doesn't
matter if it's true or just pretend.

Speaking with him truly lifted my soul. He's not
just my brother; he's also my friend.

There was something very familiar about this
man and the words that he said.

I felt as though I knew him. Maybe it was
the message he was trying spread:

That we are all brothers and sisters with
special needs to a different degree,

And we are able to help each other when
we look past color and pedigree.

He was in need of some money, and I had
extra that I could give to him.

I needed *soul lifting,* which he blessed me
with when he sang a gospel hymn.

Jesus said, "Whatever you do for the least
of my brothers, you do for Me."

My new friend touched my heart and soul in
a way that I'm grateful I can see.

Then we boarded the ferry to the Island of
Liberty—where the lady stands.

She proclaims freedom and justice as she
greets newcomers from foreign lands.

People come from all over the world to see
this statue, if even just for a peek—

To see this symbol of the freedom and
opportunity that so many of us seek.

We couldn't stay long. We were running
out of time to see other sights.

We had to choose shopping in Chinatown
or Ellis Island for new insights.

I chose to go to Chinatown because I still
needed gifts for a couple of kids.

It was so crowded and busy there, I thought
the guys just might flip their lids!

There was nowhere to get a beer that we could
see, nor a bathroom within two blocks.

It didn't take long for me to wish I had
disembarked at the Ellis Island docks.

I wouldn't say it was bad there, just not
what I expected, that's for sure,

Especially with no beer to make the ordeal
easier for the guys to endure.

Well, those are the places we saw and just some of the people we met.

But there are some things I haven't told you.
Sorry, but I'm not finished yet.

I haven't mentioned that in between all these
sights, the shopping, and all our talking,

We took cab rides, the kind you see on TV,
and did a whole lot of walking!

We ate some of the best meals ever and found
a new favorite, crème brûlée.

We also paid more than ever for our meals,
but that's because they were *gourmet.*

We searched from market to market for real
fake purses; Beth needed a Gucci.

By the end of the day, we had bags full of
bags made from genuine poochie!

And I bought a painting of the New York City
skyline while in Times Square.

I wanted to remember everything that we
did and saw while we were there.

We bought an ice cream from a Mister Softee
as we walked along the city streets,

And I thought about how thankful I was to be
blessed with these special fall treats.

If we could remember that *one nation under God*
is how our country was founded—

And if those who come here are slighted by the
faith and hope in which we are grounded—

Then we'd realize that when they ask us to take
the Lord out of our country and our hearts,

That is when *our land* becomes just like *the land
they fled,* and terror and chaos starts.

Lord God, help us to remember the days when
Your love ruled our heart, soul, and mind,

When instead of hurting and killing our brothers
and sisters, we were peaceful and kind.

Lord, please forgive us for our ignorance,
and live in our hearts once again.

Help our nation turn back to You so that we
may rest in Your precious hope. Amen.

From God's Own Word

"Blessed is the nation whose God is the Lord" (Psalms 33:12).

"Then if My people who are called by My name will humble themselves and pray and seek My face and turn from their wicked ways, I will hear from heaven and will forgive their sins and restore their land" (2 Chronicles 7:14).

"Men, you are brothers; why do you want to hurt each other" (Acts 7:18)?